Forward Through the Rearview Mirror

The MIT Press
Cambridge, Massachusetts · London, England

Reflections On and By Marshall McLuhan

Edited by Paul Benedetti and Nancy DeHart

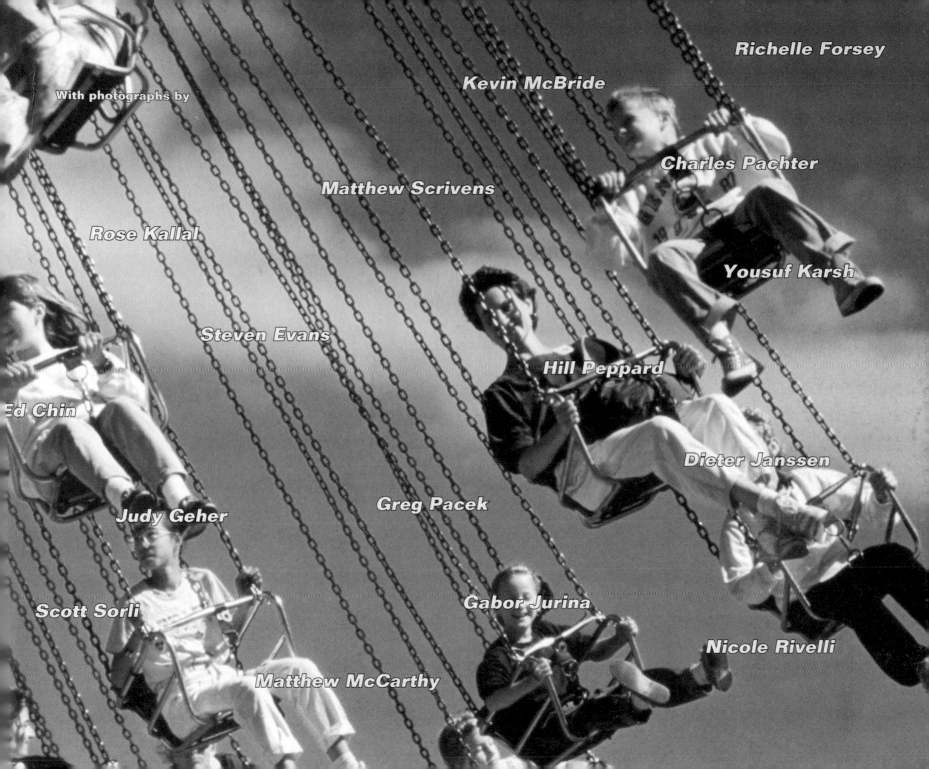

With photographs by

Richelle Forsey

Kevin McBride

Matthew Scrivens

Rose Kallal

Charles Pachter

Yousuf Karsh

Steven Evans

Ed Chin

Hill Peppard

Dieter Janssen

Greg Pacek

Judy Geher

Gabor Jurina

Scott Sorli

Nicole Rivelli

Matthew McCarthy

Contents

He repeated insistently that we should stop saying "Is this a good thing or bad thing?" and start saying, "What's going on?"

Liss Jeffrey

The electronic age... angelizes man, disembodies him. Turns him into software. Marshall McLuhan, 1971

Alleged Victim

He was a pyromaniac of the imagination, starting prairie fires over our intellectual landscape.

Patrick Watson

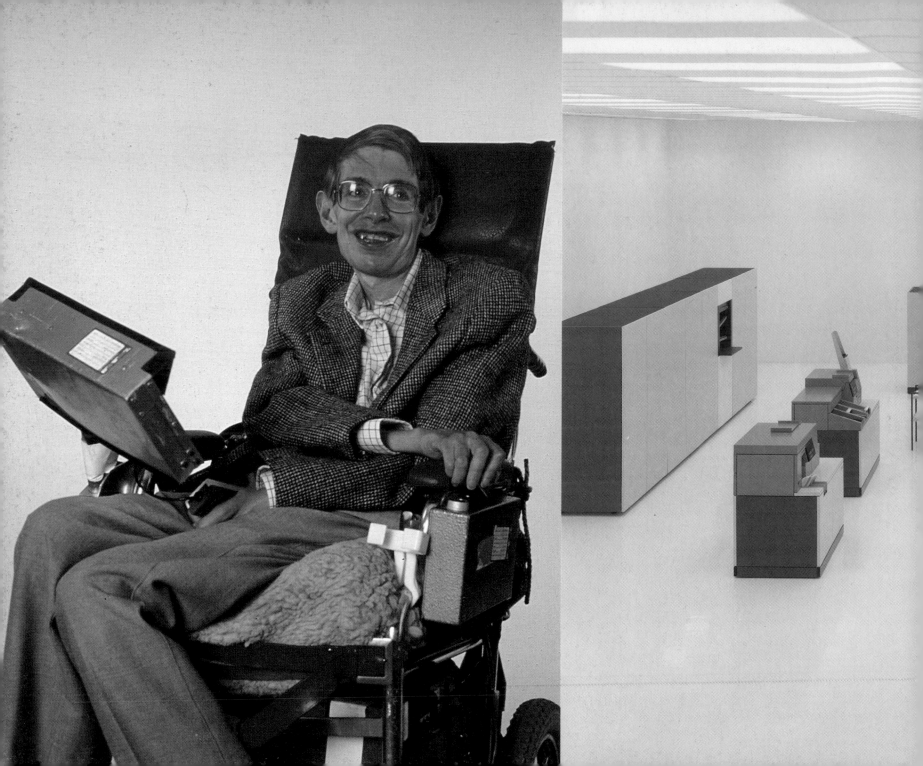

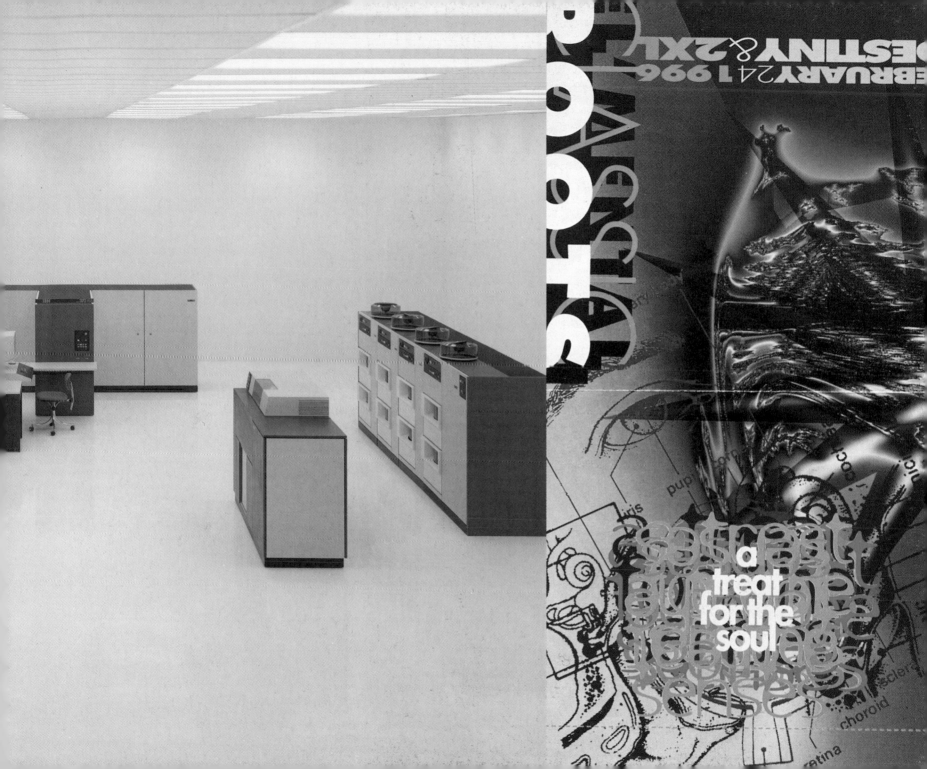

a
treat
for the
soul

Unlike previous environmental changes, the electric media constitute a total and near instantaneous transformation of culture, values and attitudes. **Marshall McLuhan, 1974**

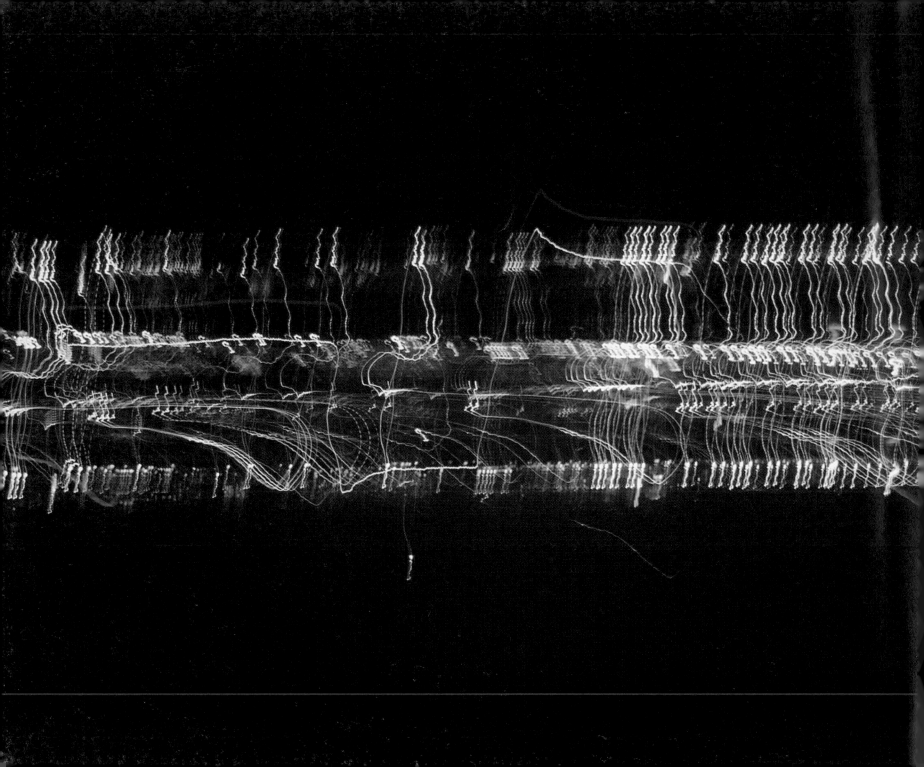

The electric media are a mom-and-child or rock-and-roll relationship.

Marshall McLuhan, 1974

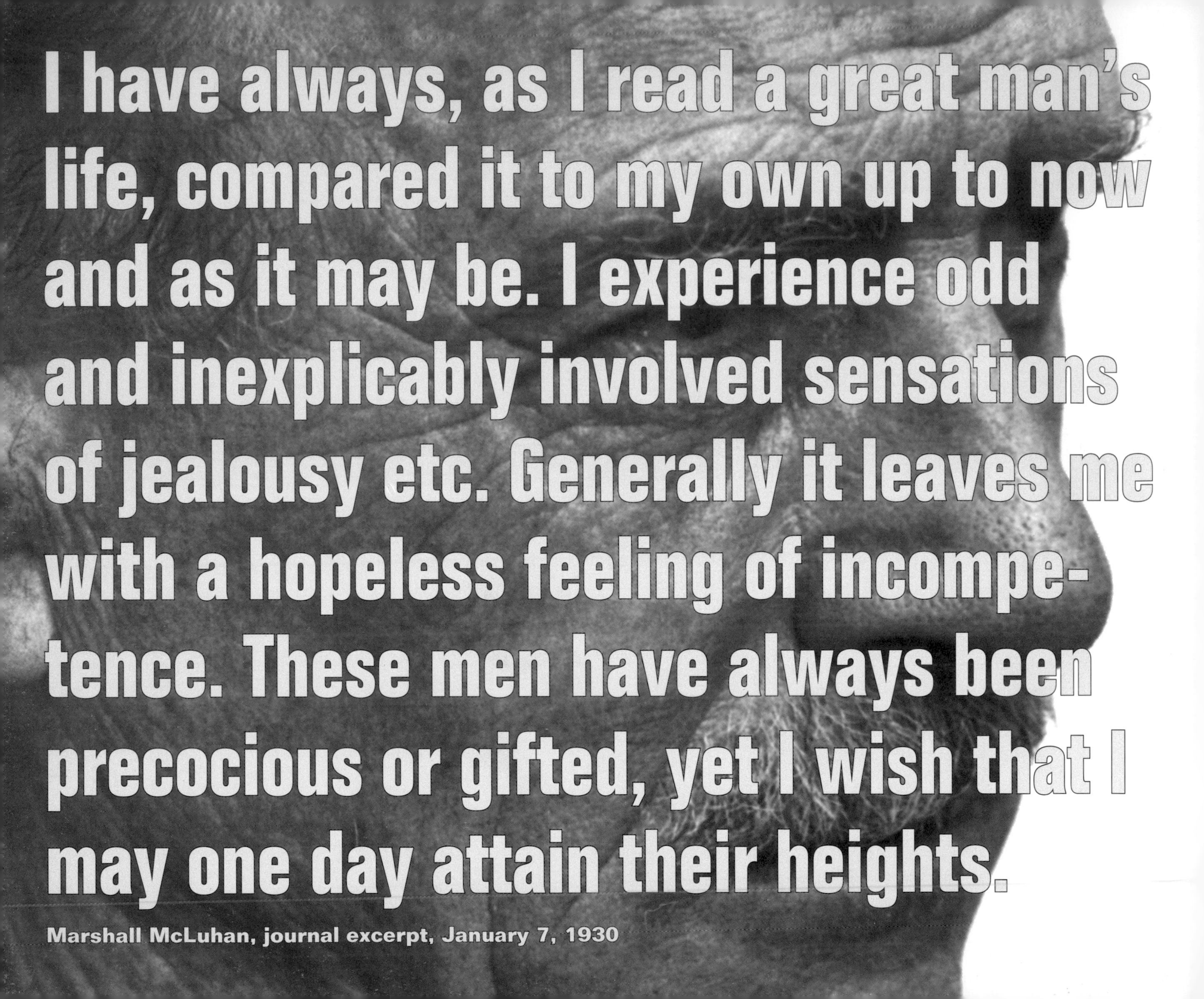

I have always, as I read a great man's life, compared it to my own up to now and as it may be. I experience odd and inexplicably involved sensations of jealousy etc. Generally it leaves me with a hopeless feeling of incompe-tence. These men have always been precocious or gifted, yet I wish that I may one day attain their heights.

Marshall McLuhan, journal excerpt, January 7, 1930

1911 Marshall McLuhan is born on July 21 in Edmonton, Alberta.

1916 McLuhan family moves to Winnipeg, Manitoba.

1923 Fails Grade 6, so Elsie McLuhan places him in Grade 7, where he excels.

1928 Enrolls at the University of Manitoba; majors in English and philosophy.

1930 Publishes his first article, "MacAulay—What a Man!" in the University of Manitoba student newspaper.
Wonders in his journal if he will contribute "a single worthy work" to mankind.

1933 Graduates with a Bachelor of Arts degree and wins the University of Manitoba gold medal in arts and science.

1934 Completes his Master of Arts degree at the University of Manitoba.
Enrolls at Trinity Hall, Cambridge University, as an undergraduate and encounters the New Criticism, which profoundly affects his intellectual life.

1936 Earns a Bachelor of Arts degree from Cambridge.
Takes a job as a teaching assistant at the University of Wisconsin for an annual salary of $895.

1937 Converts to Roman Catholicism on March 30.
Hired as an English instructor at St. Louis University, one of the finest Catholic universities in the United States.

1938 Meets Corinne Keller Lewis, a young student actress at the Pasadena Playhouse.

1939 Shortly before McLuhan's return to Cambridge, he and his bride elope on August 3. The couple honeymoon in Europe on the eve of the Second World War.

1942 The McLuhans' first child, Thomas Eric, is born in January.

1943 Receives his PhD from Cambridge.
Meets critic and painter Wyndham Lewis, beginning a friendship that lasts until Lewis's death.

1944 Accepts a job as head of the English department at Assumption College in Windsor, Ontario.

1946 Moves to Toronto, Ontario, after being invited to teach at St. Michael's College, University of Toronto. He is considered at the time to be one of Ontario's only experts in the field of modern poetry and criticism.

1951 Publishes his first book, *The Mechanical Bride: Folklore of Industrial Man*, an examination of the impact of advertising on society and culture. The book receives good reviews but sells only a few hundred copies.

1952 The McLuhans' sixth and last child, Michael, is born in October.

1953 McLuhan and Edmund Carpenter found *Explorations*, a magazine devoted to the study of language and media.

1955 Idea Consultants, a short-lived business, is established. McLuhan's ideas, including TV dinners and video movies, are prescient but unsellable.

1958 As the keynote speaker at the annual National Association of Educational Broadcasters convention in Omaha, Nebraska, McLuhan uses the phrase "the medium is the message" for the first time in a major international forum.

1959 After nine issues, the magazine *Explorations* folds, but not before creating a cultlike following around McLuhan's idea.

1960 McLuhan's report for the National Association of Educational Broadcasters is published. Though largely ignored, it will become the basis for his landmark book, *Understanding Media: The Extensions of Man*.

1962 Publishes *The Gutenberg Galaxy: The Making of Typographic Man*.

1963 McLuhan establishes the Centre for Culture and Technology in an old coach house on the University of Toronto campus. Its purpose is to examine the impact of technologies on man.

1964 Publishes *Understanding Media: The Extensions of Man*, which catapults McLuhan into the intellectual and media spotlight.

1966 McLuhan is the subject of two *New Yorker* magazine cartoons.

1967 Publishes *The Medium is the Massage: An Inventory of Effects* with Quentin Fiore and Jerome Agel, after more than a dozen publishers reject the book. It eventually sells more than one million copies worldwide.
In September, McLuhan is awarded the one-year Albert Schweitzer Chair in the Humanities at New York's Fordham University.
In November, McLuhan undergoes surgery for the removal of a benign brain tumor at Columbia Presbyterian Medical Center. He recovers, but suffers some memory loss and acute sensitivity to noise.
Makes the cover of *Newsweek* magazine.
Delivers the prestigious Marfleet Lectures at the University of Toronto.

1968 Founds the *McLuhan Dew-Line* newsletter in an attempt to sell his ideas to the business community.
Publication of *War and Peace in the Global Village* with Quentin Fiore and Jerome Agel.
Publishes *Through The Vanishing Point: Space in Poetry and Painting* with Harley Parker.

1969 Publishes *Counterblast* with Harley Parker.

1970 Publishes *Culture Is Our Business*.
Publishes *From Cliché to Archetype* with Wilfred Watson.
Appointed as a Companion of the Order of Canada.

1972 Publication of *Take Today: The Executive as Dropout* with Barrington Nevitt.

1973 The Vatican appoints McLuhan as an advisor on social communications.

1976 Suffers a minor stroke after the filming of a short scene in the Woody Allen movie, *Annie Hall*.

1977 Publishes *City as Classroom: Understanding Language and Media* with Eric McLuhan and Kathryn Hutchon.

1979 In September, McLuhan suffers a massive stroke that leaves him unable to speak more than a few words at a time.

1980 Without McLuhan to head the Centre for Culture and Technology, the University of Toronto decides to close it.
On December 31, McLuhan dies in his sleep.

1988 Publication of *Laws of the Media: The New Science* by Eric and Marshall McLuhan.

1989 Publication of *The Global Village* by Marshall McLuhan and Bruce Powers.
Publication of *Marshall McLuhan: The Medium and the Messenger*, a biography of McLuhan by Philip Marchand.

1993 *Wired* magazine is founded; McLuhan is named "patron saint" of the popular high-tech periodical.

1996 Release of *Understanding McLuhan*, the first multimedia CD-ROM about Marshall McLuhan.

CENTRE
FOR
CULTURE
AND
TECHNOLOGY

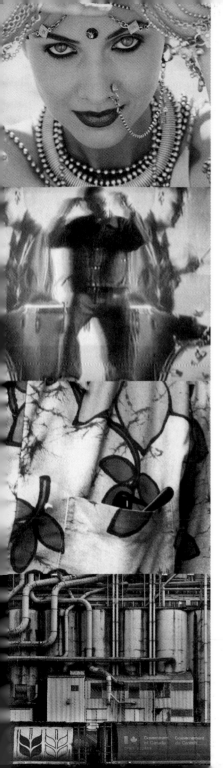

Introduction

Herbert Marshall McLuhan, world-renowned media theorist, loved wordplay. An inveterate punster and master of aphorism and the art of rhetoric, McLuhan revelled in verbal gymnastics. On a television show in 1967, McLuhan told a befuddled interviewer, "The urb it orbs," and "The new clothing of the planet is garbage." Such emphatic, epigrammatic pronouncements were deliberately opaque and common for McLuhan. The Cambridge-educated, University of Toronto professor delighted in provoking thought and stimulating new ideas among his students, readers, and listeners. "My father decided early on that he would try as much as he could to write and present his ideas in aphoristic style," said McLuhan's son and collaborator, Eric. "It's a poetic form. And it calls for a lot of participation on the part of the person regarding it or thinking about it."

It is hardly surprising then that in 1967 when McLuhan declared that "the future of the future is the present," his comment was met with universal bewilderment. In typical cryptic style, he suggested, "If you are really curious about the future, just study the present.... What we ordinarily see in any present is really what appears in the rearview mirror. What we ordinarily think of as present is really past." For many of his detractors, this was just another bit of "McLuhanacy," easily dismissed and forgotten. However, like his famous phrases, "the medium is the message" and "global village," his notion of the "rearview mirror" is one of the most important insights McLuhan left us to help understand our age.

McLuhan recognized that most people live in the rearview mirror — moving ahead in time, but actually living in the past. "People never want to live in the present," he said. "People live in the rearview mirror because it's safer.... They've been there before, they feel comfortable." For McLuhan, the key to understanding the future was simply to focus on the present. As this book's title suggests, by looking back to McLuhan we find the tools we need to analyze the present and look forward into our future.

During his own time, McLuhan accurately perceived the present and illuminated the future in a series of provocative books. He was catapulted into the media spotlight in 1964 with the publication of *Understanding Media: The Extensions of Man.* Idolized by undergraduates, sought after by journalists, featured on the cover of *Newsweek,* spoofed in *New Yorker* cartoons, and extolled in major newspapers for his trenchant observations on how the tools we shape shape us, McLuhan was, for a brief time, one of the world's most celebrated minds. Tom Wolfe called McLuhan "the most important thinker since Newton, Darwin, Freud, Einstein and Pavlov"; Norman Mailer suggested McLuhan's discussions of "the medium is the message" and the "global village" were among "the most useful remarks of the twentieth century." By the mid-seventies, however, McLuhan's fame had peaked, and through the rest of the decade his popularity and influence waned. Overexposure in the media, a string of books that garnered little critical acclaim, and a shifting political climate sidelined McLuhan. By the time of his death in 1980, McLuhan's Centre for Culture and Technology at the University of Toronto was shut down, most of his books were out of print, and little was heard outside of academic circles about his work.

By the early nineties, however, McLuhan's reputation was once again on the rise. The world began experiencing a media revolution unparalleled since the introduction of the Gutenberg printing press. People started rereading McLuhan and discovered that a quarter of a century before words such as *on-line*, *wired*, and *the Web* became part of our vocabulary, they existed in McLuhan's lexicon. More than a decade after his death, we go back to McLuhan and move forward through the rearview mirror to find a startling series of theories on the effects of media on culture and society. As Eric McLuhan says, his father left us a "set of answers to questions that nobody else asks and nobody else answers."

Forward Through the Rearview Mirror is a collection of some of these questions and answers that help us perceive the patterns of our present and future. McLuhan rejected a content-based approach to understanding technology. As his biographer Philip Marchand writes, McLuhan embraced "a comprehensive, effects-oriented approach — an attempt to grasp the whole pattern of change, including the innumerable and often ignored side effects of technological development." When it came to books, McLuhan eschewed the traditional literary format. He rejected linearity, sequential advancement of argument, and a sustained point of view. In the *Gutenberg Galaxy: The Making of Typographic Man* — a book with no chapters, just 279 pages of type punctuated by bold-faced quotations — McLuhan used what he called "a mosaic or field approach." Similarly, in *Understanding Media*, though there are chapters, there is no discernible progress from beginning to end.

In *Forward Through the Rearview Mirror*, we have adapted the method and sensibility of McLuhan's approach. Having worked on a team that had produced the CD-ROM *Understanding McLuhan*, we had come to comprehend the concepts of non-linearity and a medium that offers multiple points of view. The language of multimedia is hauntingly similar to McLuhan's three-decade-old notion of a "field approach." Consequently, this book is a "mosaic" of text by McLuhan, biographical vignettes, photos, commentary, and reminiscences about McLuhan. Although clarity is brought to the material through three distinct typographic treatments — all material written by McLuhan is in blue, material written about McLuhan is in black, and biographical text is italicized — there is no one way to read this volume. When reading McLuhan, as his associate Derrick de Kerckhove explains, it is necessary to play "experience and knowledge against these new combinations of thoughts that arise from these new bits and pieces of writing. You are the bond of the thoughts — you, the reader."

Also in keeping with McLuhan's sensibility, this book combines text and images in a design that is appropriate to his aphoristic style and encourages understanding of the man many found incomprehensible. This approach takes its cue from another of McLuhan's publications:

the 1967 landmark collaboration between designer Quentin Fiore and producer Jerome Agel, who used selections from McLuhan's writings to create a radically new kind of book, titled *The Medium is the Massage: An Inventory of Effects*. An astonishing swirl of images, photographs, text, typography, and layout, *Massage's* unconventional format was part book, part magazine, part storyboard, designed to stimulate — intellectually, visually, and emotionally — without a fixed beginning or end.

The material in *Forward Through the Rearview Mirror* is organized into four sections — Global Village, Violence and Identity, Medium is the Message, and Extensions of Man. These chapters attempt to convey McLuhan's central concepts, which are by their nature neither definable nor containable. The excerpts were chosen to give readers an introduction to McLuhan's vast body of work, particularly to those ideas with contemporary significance. However, in keeping with what McLuhan wrote to journalist Robert Fulford — "I do not move along lines. I use points like dots in a wire photo. That is why I must repeat and repeat my points." — no idea, no sentence, and no phrase in the book stands alone. This book is a compilation of McLuhan's theories that inexorably echo, circle, and shift into one another.

In describing his friend, Patrick Watson said that McLuhan "was not an analyst, not a historian, not a sociologist, but a poet. What he was delivering to the world was a set of metaphors that we had to wrestle with, that worked at the essential metaphoric level of poetry." Like McLuhan's own poetic approach, the selection, juxtaposition, and collision of images and text are sometimes explanatory, sometimes evocative, and occasionally may generate new and surprising rereadings of McLuhan's words. The anecdotes and commentary by notable writers, critics, and colleagues of McLuhan are presented to offer a view of the man behind the aphorisms. Though divergent in their opinions, these commentators agree that to some extent time has caught up with McLuhan, that many of his ideas are more understandable today than they were three decades ago.

In going back to McLuhan, we find no absolute understanding of the man or of the forces that were changing his world and continue to change ours. McLuhan promised no such clarity. In his probing of media, he offered us a technique for understanding our time and the forces that shape it. He wrote, "I began to realize that the greatest artists of the 20th Century — Yeats, Pound, Joyce, Eliot — discovered a totally different approach, based on the identity of the processes of cognition and creation. I realized that artistic creation is the playback of ordinary experience — from trash to treasures. I ceased being a moralist and became a student." Perhaps McLuhan's greatest legacy is that he challenges us to examine the present, he exhorts us to study the effects of media on our lives and our world — to be eternal students.

Paul Benedetti and Nancy DeHart
August 1996

Electrically speaking, there's nothing but nuzzling and cuddling and cooing, alternating with wild yells for love and food and help. It's always May Day in the global nursery.

Marshall McLuhan, "Making Contact with Marshall McLuhan," interview by Louis Forsdale, 1974

Global Village

THERE ARE NO REMOTE PLACES.

Under instant circuitry, nothing is remote in time or in space. It's now. Marshall McLuhan, *Take Thirty*, CBC Television, 1965

Ann Landers

Today, the instantaneous world of electric information media involves all of us, all at once. Ours is a brand-new world of all-at-onceness. Time, in a sense, has ceased and space has vanished. Like primitives, we now live in a global village of our own making, a simultaneous happening. The global village is not created by the motor car or even by the airplane. It is created by instant electronic information movement. The global village is at once as wide as the planet and as small as the little town where everybody is maliciously engaged in poking his nose into everybody else's business. The global village is a world in which you don't necessarily have harmony; you have extreme concern with everybody else's business and much involvement in everybody else's life. It's a sort of Ann Landers column written larger. And it doesn't necessarily mean harmony and peace and quiet, but it does mean huge involvement in everybody else's affairs. And so, the global village is as big as a planet and as small as the village post office.

We now share too much about each other to be strangers to each other. For example, in the age of the information explosion, all the walls go out between age-groups, between family groups, national groups, between economies. The walls all go out. People suddenly have to adjust themselves to this new proximity, this new interrelationship, and merely to tell them that this has happened isn't very helpful. What they need to know is, if it is happening, what does it mean to me?

Marshall McLuhan, "McLuhan on McLuhanism," WNDT Educational Broadcasting Network, 1966

TELECOMMUNICATION BREAKDOWN

EBN

The work of Marshall McLuhan, like the work of many noted intellectual explorers, owed as much to force of character as intellect. His restless energy, his impatience with dullness and routine, his delight in subverting cherished notions of both the right and the left, his showmanship, his old-fashioned piety, even his occasional flirtation with paranoia and superstition — these qualities shaped his thought. ⊙

McLuhan always struck me as being exceptional. Not just because of what he was saying: I think it had to do with the level of existence that he settled in on once and for all. I range from being familial to professional, to chummy, to having moments of illumination and reflection. I never saw McLuhan step below a fairly high level of business. That was the lowest depth for him. What I call a fairly high level of thinking and involvement with reality — that was the ground floor for McLuhan. He could only see up from there. Below it, he was incompetent. The media made this painfully clear: it showed how oddly he dealt with the wedding of his daughter; how his brother described him as being completely out of it. McLuhan was the proverbial idiot savant. His head was elsewhere. That is a function of personality. It has to be. **Derrick de Kerckhove**

Loaded With Data

We have laid out our own electric networks on a global scale by cables, by telegrams, by radio, by all sorts of electric means. These circuits are loaded with data that move instantly and that have become indispensible to all decision-making in the Western world in business, in education, and in politics. Marshall McLuhan, *Take Thirty*, CBC Television, 1965

Marshall McLuhan photographed by Yousuf Karsh, 1967.

Aphorisms

McLuhan's writings may not provide all the answers to our most pressing questions. If nothing else, however, the style of his work—its spirit of playful, free-ranging inquiry—may well serve as inspiration to the intellectual explorers of our own age. ⊙

My father decided in the sixties that he would try as much as he could to present his ideas in an aphoristic style. Aphorisms, as Francis Bacon said, are incomplete, a bit like cartoons. They are not filled-out essay writing that is highly compressed. The aphorism is a poetic form that calls for a lot of participation on the part of the reader. You have to chew on an aphorism and work with it for a while before you understand it fully. A good aphorism could keep you busy for a week—kicking it around, playing with it, exploring it, taking it apart to see what you can get out of it. And applying it here, there, and everywhere. My father deliberately chose this form of statement because he wanted to teach, not tell or entertain. He said, "For instruction, you use incomplete knowledge so people can fill things in—they can round it out and fill it in with their own experience." If what you want to do is simply to tell people something, then by all means spell it out in the connected essay. But if you want to teach, you don't do that. There's no participation in just telling: that's simply for consumers—they sit there and swallow it, or not. But the aphoristic style gives you the opportunity to get a dialogue going, to engage people in the process of discovery. **Eric McLuhan**

Left to right: Mother and child, Elsie and Marshall McLuhan in 1912; McLuhan at Cambridge in the early forties; Marshall and Corinne McLuhan in 1958 with their children Eric, Teresa, Mary, Stephanie, Elizabeth, and Michael; seventies embrace: Corinne and Marshall in their Wychwood Park garden.

The new environment of simultaneous and diversified information creates acoustic man. He is surrounded by sound — from behind, from the side, from above. His environment is made up of information in all kinds of simultaneous forms, and he puts on this electrical environment as we put on our clothes, or as the fish puts on water. Marshall McLuhan, "McLuhan probe," original source and date unknown

Bump, Babble, Gossip

Transmitted at the speed of light, all events on this planet are simultaneous. In the electric environment of information, all events are simultaneous. There is no time or space separating events. Information and images bump against each other every day in massive quantities, and the resonance of this interfacing is like the babble of a village or tavern gossip session. The absence of space brings to mind the idea of a village. But actually, at the speed of light, the planet is not much bigger than this room we're in. In terms of time and the speed of the events that are now programmed, they hit each other so fast that even a village is too big a thing to use for comparison. The acoustic or simultaneous space in which we now live is like a sphere whose center is everywhere and whose margins are nowhere. Acoustic space cannot be cut into pieces, as visual space can. It is both compressed and indivisible.

Marshall McLuhan, "Making Contact with Marshall McLuhan," interview by Louis Forsdale, 1974

In the electric age we wear all mankind as our skin.

Marshall McLuhan, *Understanding Media*, 1964

Tribalism

1911 *Herbert Marshall McLuhan was born on July 21, 1911, in Edmonton, Alberta, to Herbert McLuhan and Elsie Hall McLuhan. Herbert McLuhan was a genial, easygoing man who had come west with his father and brothers from Ontario to homestead on the prairie. Elsie Hall's family had come from Nova Scotia for the same purpose. Unfortunately, Elsie's father, Henry Seldon Hall, was bad-tempered and abusive, and Elsie, as a wife and mother, bore the scars of her upbringing. She was high-strung, willful and ambitious, and quarreled frequently with her husband, whose career as a life insurance salesman was only modestly successful. ⊙*

Since the telegraph and radio the globe has contracted, spatially, into a single large village. Tribalism is our only resource since the electromagnetic discovery.

Marshall McLuhan, *The Gutenberg Galaxy*, 1962

The alphabet (and its extension into typography) made possible the spread of the power that is knowledge and shattered the bonds of tribal man, thus exploding him into an agglomeration of individuals. Electric writing and speed pour upon him instantaneously and continuously the concerns of all other men. He becomes tribal once more. The human family becomes one tribe again.

Marshall McLuhan, *Understanding Media*, 1964

Herbert Marshall McLuhan's birth announcement, handwritten by his father.

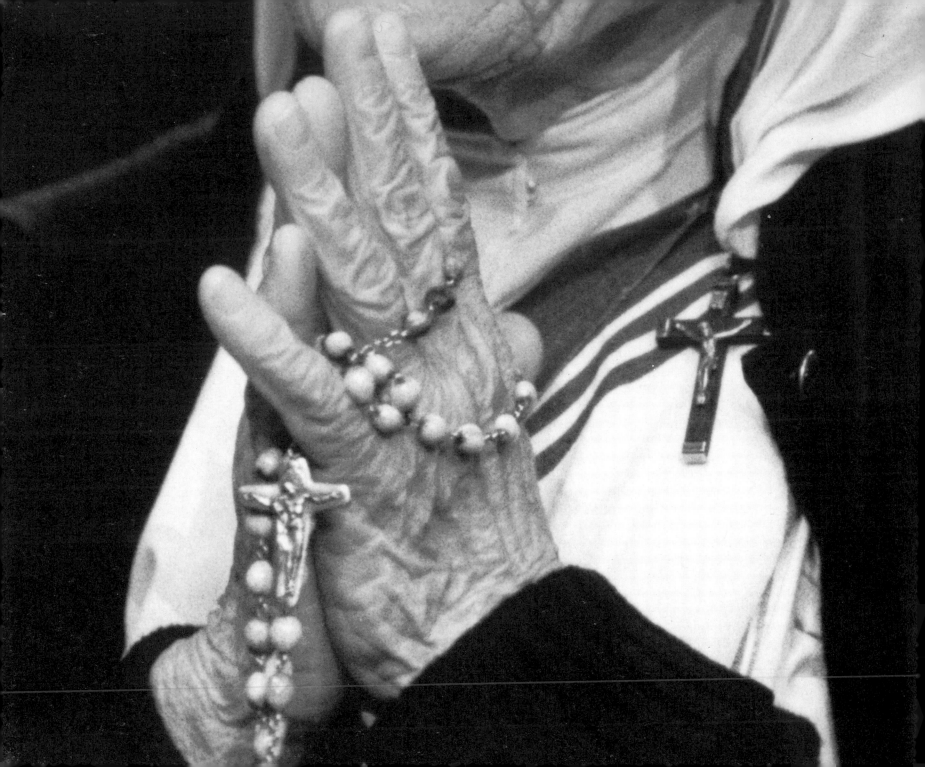

1920

Like many another boy favored by a mother who dominates a household, McLuhan—he had only one sibling, a younger brother, Maurice, who took after his father—was himself of a domineering, ambitious temperament. He also inherited a striking verbal facility from his mother, who was an elocutionist and often performed dramatic monologues in church halls. As an adult, McLuhan was far more compelling as a speaker than a writer and could hold forth in front of audiences for hours. ⊙

Acoustic space is created by our ability to hear from all directions at once. Electric information arrives from all quarters at once. Thus, in effect, acoustic environments were created by the telegraph and began to show up in the press as mosaics of juxtaposed and discontinuous items all under one dateline. Acoustic space is all touch and interplay, all resonance and sympathy. Acoustic space is like the relationship of mother and child, which is audile-tactile, sound and touch. The cooing and handling and touching—this is the kind of world the electric media put around us. The electric media are a mom-and-child or rock-and-roll relationship.

Marshall McLuhan, "Making Contact with Marshall McLuhan," interview by Louis Forsdale, 1974

Today, in the jet age, every city in the world is a suburban satellite to every other city. The only possible regional environment for existing or prospective cities, large or small, is the planet itself.

Marshall McLuhan and Barrington Nevitt, *Take Today: The Executive as Dropout*, 1972

Left: a promotional poster advertising Elsie McLuhan's public recitals;
right: Elsie and Marshall at the beach.

1921

The McLuhan family, after a series of moves prompted by economic woes and the dislocation caused by the First World War, settled in a modest, middle-class area of Winnipeg, Manitoba, in 1921. McLuhan entered the University of Manitoba in 1928, where he majored in English and philosophy—a natural course for a young man brought up in a household that, however divided by emotional conflicts, was united in its reverence for books and education. McLuhan, with a few exceptions, found his teachers inadequate and suspected, rightly, that he was receiving a second-rate education.

The most lasting intellectual experience from this period of McLuhan's life was his discovery of the English essayist Gilbert Keith Chesterton. Chesterton's intellectual agility, his love of paradox and wordplay, and his defense of the Catholic Church and rejection of modernity made a profound impact on McLuhan, who would convert to Catholicism in 1937. In later years, McLuhan was fond of saying that, as a young man, he detested the modern age—finding ammunition for his views not only in Chesterton but in such Radical Tory writers of the nineteenth century as Thomas Carlyle and John Ruskin. Although McLuhan never lost his distaste for the modern age, he eventually realized his only defense was to try to understand it—especially its media of communication. ⊙

Deep Into The Night

One of the most memorable times I spent with McLuhan was at a meeting in Cincinnati of the National Council of Teachers of English. I remember that Charlie Weingartner, McLuhan, and I shared a room together, which was great fun because Charlie and I had a chance to listen to him invent ideas and do his probes deep into the night. On that occasion, his cigar was lit and the lights were off and it was two or three in the morning, and we finally had to ask him if he could stop and let us all get some sleep. **Neil Postman**

A tribal and feudal hierarchy of the traditional kind collapses quickly when it meets any hot medium of the mechanical, uniform, and repetitive kind. The medium of money or wheel or writing, or any other form of specialist speed-up of exchange and information, will serve to fragment a tribal structure. Similarly, a very much greater speed-up, such as occurs with electricity, may serve to restore a tribal pattern of intense involvement such as took place with the introduction of radio in Europe, and is now tending to happen as a result of TV in America. Specialist technologies detribalize. The nonspecialist electric technology retribalizes.

Marshall McLuhan, *Understanding Media*, 1964

1934 *After completing an MA in English at the University of Manitoba in 1934, McLuhan went to Cambridge to study English. It was the most fortunate move he could have made.*

At Cambridge, such luminaries as I. A. Richards and F. R. Leavis were pioneering the approach to literature known as the New Criticism. Earlier criticism of poetry, while it pointed out the beauties of diction, rhythm, and sound, had tended to look upon individual poems as the expression of the ideas and personality of the poet. I. A. Richards, however, was concerned primarily with how the poem communicated meaning—not meaning in the sense of concepts that could be paraphrased, but states of mind and emotion. He emphasized that most words had several different meanings, and that the meaning of a word in a poem varied according to its context. The trick, then, was to pay close attention to every word in a poem, to juggle possible meanings, and to decide intelligently which ones made the most sense. ☉

Left: McLuhan (back row, middle) with his Trinity Hall rowing team in the thirties; *right*: McLuhan's PhD from Cambridge University, December 1943.

With electronics, any marginal area can become center, and marginal experiences can be had at any center. Perhaps the city needed to coordinate and concert the distracted sense programs of our global village will have to be built by computers in the way in which a big airport has to coordinate multiple flights.

Marshall McLuhan, letter to Jacqueline Tyrwhitt, 1960

Repeat-Repeat-Repeat

And so, as we sit here at the top of Sutton Place, what suddenly strikes the viewer is an enormous amount of cave-dwelling art. Apartments in a high-rise building are a little repeat-repeat-repeat module that create exactly the form that Andy Warhol called mini-art. When you repeat the apartment form hundreds and hundreds of times in a small space, such as these high rises, you really switch into a tribal or cave world. And these people, therefore—I hadn't realized it really until we sat here a few minutes ago—these people in these new types of cave dwellings really depend upon electric information for their existence. Electric elevators, electric telephones, electric TV, electric radio. Without these electric services this sort of cave world would be impossible.

Marshall McLuhan, *W5*, CTV Television, 1969

Lines Of Force

Men live in round houses until they become sedentary and specialized in their work organization. Anthropologists have often noted this change from round to square without knowing its cause. The media analyst can help the anthropologist in this matter, although the explanation will not be obvious to people of visual culture. The visual man, likewise, cannot see much difference between the motion picture and TV, or between a Corvair and a Volkswagen, for this difference is not between two visual spaces, but between tactile and visual ones. A tent or a wigwam is not an enclosed or visual space. Neither is a cave nor a hole in the ground. These kinds of space — the tent, the wigwam, the igloo, the cave — are not enclosed in the visual sense because they follow dynamic lines of force, like a triangle. When enclosed, or translated into visual space, architecture tends to lose its tactile kinetic pressure. A square is the enclosure of a visual space; that is, it consists of space properties abstracted from manifest tensions. A triangle follows lines of force, this being the most economical way of anchoring a vertical object. A square moves beyond such kinetic pressures to enclose visual space relations while depending upon diagonal anchors. This separation of the visual from direct tactile and kinetic pressure, and its translation into new dwelling spaces, occurs only when men have learned to practice specialization of their senses and fragmentation of their work skills. The square room or house speaks the language of the sedentary specialist, while the round hut or igloo, like the conical wigwam, tells of the integral nomadic ways of food-gathering communities. Marshall McLuhan, *Understanding Media*, 1964

McLuhan's strong points often had a flip side. As a Catholic, he was influenced by the official philosophy of the church—Saint Thomas Aquinas's view of things, which says that the universe is intelligible. In other words, our senses and our reason work together to give us a trustworthy account of the universe, so we're not misled. Therefore, McLuhan felt you could trust the patterns you saw—that there was basically an order in the world, and although it wasn't a visual diagram, it was a deeply logical system. He believed that if you recognized patterns you were onto something, you didn't have to wait for decades and decades of scientific research to figure out whether the order or the coherence of the patterns you saw was a truthful one. I think he was saying you could basically trust your perceptions.

The flip side is that he almost had a compulsion to see order and to make patterns, to see patterns and sometimes to impose patterns. So for every fad that came along—if you told McLuhan, "Gee, there are a lot of westerns on television," or "Gee, women really like these mesh stockings now," or if today, for example, you said, "Gee, the kids are wearing these big baggy pants and they love basketball and they love big air shoes"—he had a theory. He'd say, "Oh, yes, yes," and he'd think about that for a while and come out with a theory. Today, when you read some of these musings—for example, the one about the westerns on television; he said, "Westerns are wonderfully suited for television because . . ." (it was something to do with the texture, the leather)—they seem irrelevant. Westerns, of course, are long gone. **Philip Marchand**

1936 *McLuhan wrote his final exams at Cambridge in 1936 and received good, although not distinguished, marks. Returning to North America, he landed a job as a teaching assistant at the University of Wisconsin. Meanwhile, he worked on his doctoral thesis for Cambridge, which was eventually finished and accepted in 1943. The thesis was an examination of the trivium, the medieval curriculum consisting of logic, grammar, and rhetoric.*

McLuhan was fascinated by the Renaissance humanists, such as Erasmus and Sir Thomas More, who led the revolt against the Scholastic philosophers of the late Middle Ages, a period when logic was supreme. Like modern-day deconstructionism, late-medieval logic was ultra-subtle, full of jargon, and disdainful of elegant verbal style. In other words, it had almost crowded rhetoric and grammar out of the curriculum. For McLuhan, grammar, or the study of language, was nothing less than an earlier version of his cherished New Criticism. But he was also interested in the specialty of More and Erasmus, which was rhetoric—the use of language to sway an audience.

McLuhan soon noticed that modern-day advertisers were using exactly the same techniques as the ancient rhetoricians. When he taught freshman English at Wisconsin, he showed advertisements to his classes and analyzed their rhetorical devices. Throughout his career, McLuhan insisted that advertising was one of the great art forms of the age. Advertisers knew instinctively that their job was not to convey an idea or a concept, but to achieve an effect—just as poets know that they must use language to create the kind of effect they want. Although he hated the corrupt use of art in advertising, McLuhan nonetheless insisted that we should pay serious attention to advertisements. Only then would they lose their power over us. ⊙

Patterns

We have taken print culture for granted for over two thousand years, and then suddenly it all ended with our abrupt entry into an electric world of circuitry in which all of the careful organization and continuous and connected patterns were suddenly interrupted by instant circuits that involved us not just in ourselves, but in everybody. Marshall McLuhan, *Take Thirty*, CBC Television, 1965

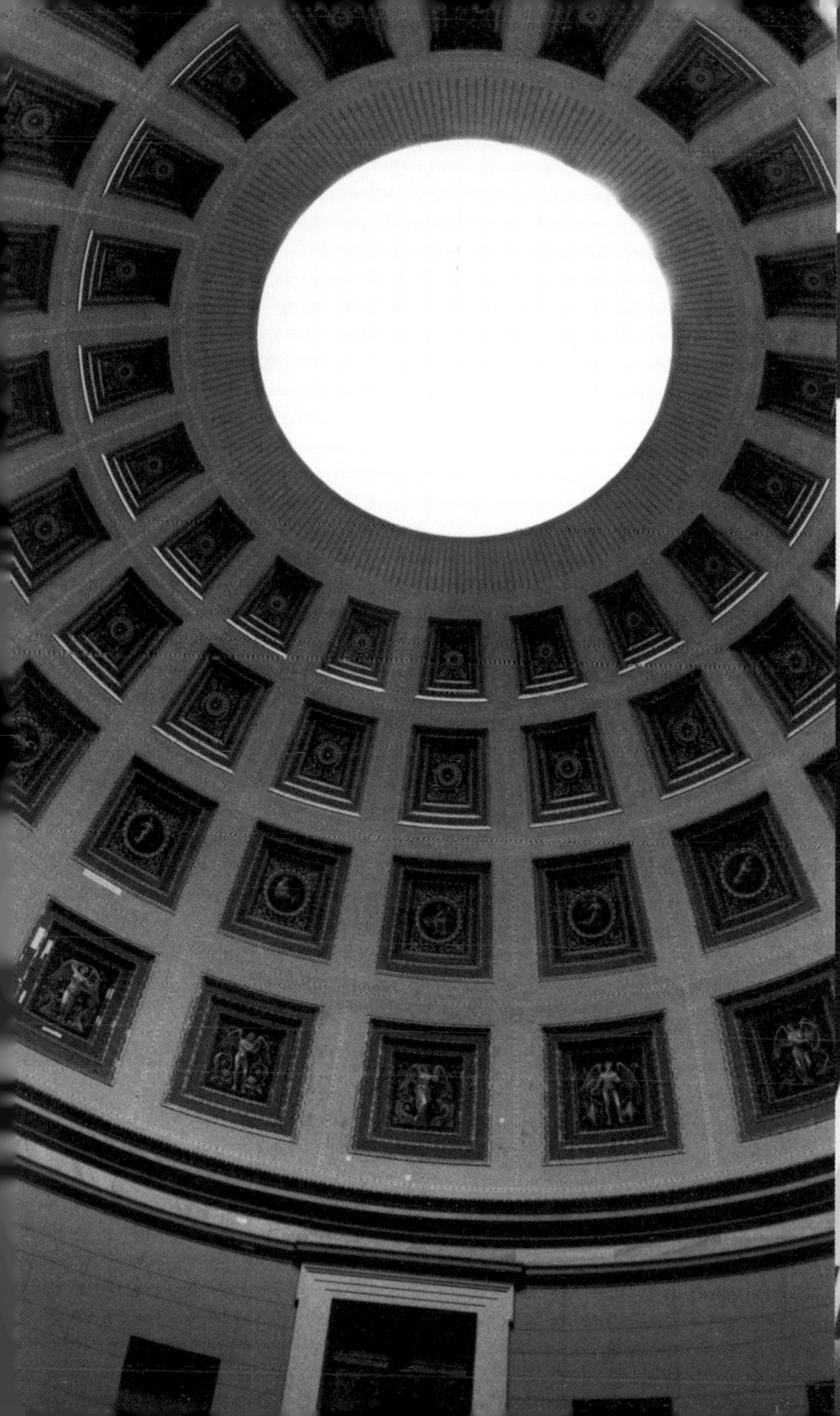

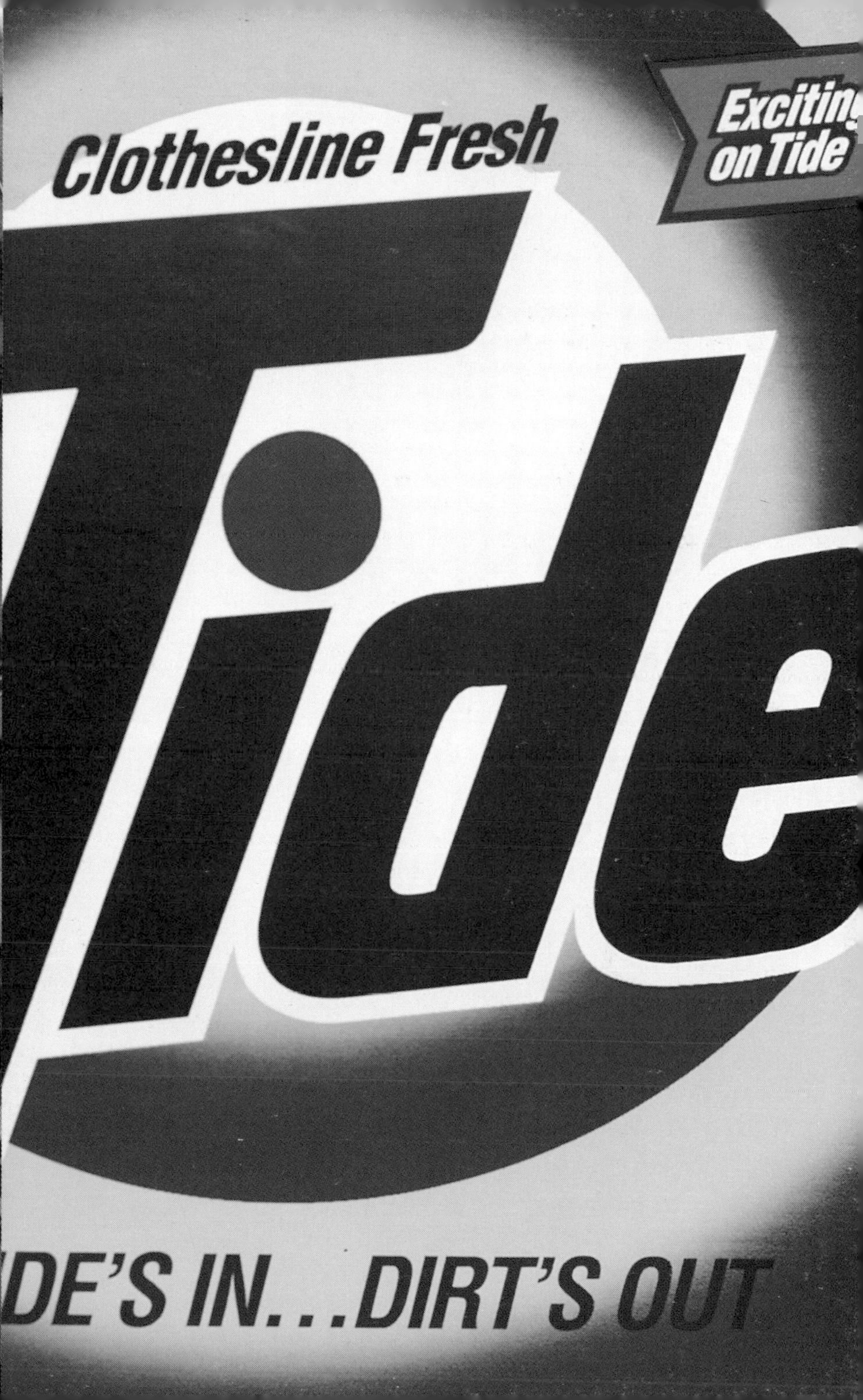
Clothesline Fresh
Exciting
on Tide
Tide
IDE'S IN...DIRT'S OUT

When McLuhan first came out with the idea of a global village in 1964, many of us did not live in a global village. Oh, yes, we took an airplane to Europe, and we were hip, we drank French wine, but we had not yet experienced instantaneous communication. The genius of McLuhan is that he saw the global village before anyone else.

With the microcomputer revolution people experienced the ideas McLuhan was talking about. These ideas are no longer theories. They are things that we live day by day. We saw the speed with which developments were taking place. We lived the information revolution and began to realize that McLuhan's ideas meant something. We discovered for ourselves the ideas of McLuhan as a pop guru who told Madison Avenue how to do its ads. We realized that McLuhan understood our age when he revealed to us that we live in a global village.

Robert Logan

The New World

The point of the matter of speed-up by wheel, road, and paper is the extension of power in an ever more homogeneous and uniform space. Thus, the real potential of the Roman technology was not realized until printing had given road and wheel a much greater speed than that of the Roman vortex. Yet the speed-up of the electronic age is as disrupting for literate, lineal, and Western man as the Roman paper routes were for tribal villagers. Our speed-up today is not a slow explosion outward from center to margins but an instant implosion and an interfusion of space and functions. Our specialist and fragmented civilization of center-margin structure is suddenly experiencing an instantaneous reassembling of all its mechanized bits into an organic whole. This is the new world of the global village.

Marshall McLuhan, *Understanding Media,* 1964

The UN is giving free transistor radios to all the backward countries in the world. The effect is to release enormous tribal violence, because it intensifies all the activity of their ear culture — the culture by which they live already. It's like pouring firewater into an Indian community. Radio in the Near East, radio in Africa is an immediate cause of violence because it steps up their sense of themselves and their interfaces among themselves to a very high pitch.

Marshall McLuhan, *The New Majority with Ed Fitzgerald*, CBC Television, 1970

I used to talk about the global village; I now speak of it more properly as the global theater. Every kid is now concerned with acting. Doing his thing outside and raising a ruckus in a quest for identity. He has lost his identity. Every child on the planet since TV has lost his identity and so becomes a violent force — a lumpen-proletariat of Marxist violence. Marshall McLuhan, *W5*, CTV Television, 1969

A moral point of view too often serves as a substitute for understanding in technological matters.

Marshall McLuhan, *Understanding Media,* 1964

Tokyo isn't much farther away than the suburbs in point of time. So the patterns of human association vary enormously with the amount of acceleration possible. I think now of the city as the planet itself, the urban village or global village. And, in fact, you could say that with the satellite, the global village has become a global theater, with everybody on the planet simultaneously participating as actors. Students around the globe feel an entire unity among themselves; they feel a homogeneity of interest. They live in an information environment created by electricity. They share the same information or electric environment of information and they share the same outlook around the world.

Marshall McLuhan, *The New Majority with Ed Fitzgerald,* CBC Television, 1970

Radio provides a speed-up of information that also causes acceleration in other media. It certainly contracts the world to village size and creates insatiable village tastes for gossip, rumor, and personal malice.

Marshall McLuhan, *Understanding Media,* 1964

Top-left window:

`http://www.theslot.com/ali/`

New? | What's Cool? | Handbook | Net Search | Net Directory | Software

MUHAMMAD ALI

The Greatest Web Site

By Bill Walsh

Top-right window:

Location: `http://www.zpub.com/un/pope/`

What's New? | What's Cool? | Handbook | Net Search | Net Directory | Software

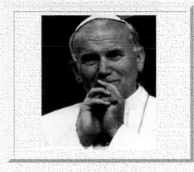

The "UNOFFICIAL"
Pope John Paul II

The Official Vatican Web Site - _Writings/Speeches_ - _Resources_ - _Food for Thought_

Pope John Paul II (1920-) is said to be the most recognized person in the world. He is the _most traveled_ Pope in the 2,000 year history of the Church and speaks eight languages. Born Karol Joseph Wojtyla (pronounced Voy-tee-wah) in Wadowice, Poland on May 18, 1920 to an administrative offic in the Polish army and a former schoolteacher. In 1978, at the age of 58 the College of Cardinals elected him to lead the Roman Catholic Church. He was the first non-italian chosen as Pope in 456 years and the youngest in this century. He is the 264th Pope from a _long list of Popes_. At age 61 he suffered serious wounds during an assassination attempt. _"Amazing Facts"_ about the Pope.

1920 - Born in Poland on May 18 - _A short Biographical Sketch_
1946 - Ordained a priest

Bottom-left window:

Forward | Home | Reload | Images | Open | Print | Find | Stop

`http://www.schwarzenegger.com/`

New? | What's Cool? | Handbook | Net Search | Net Directory | Software

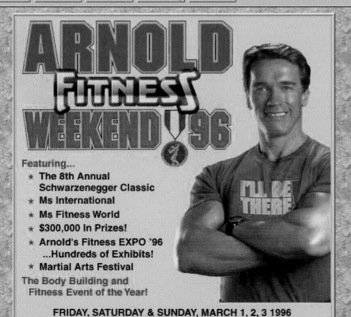

ARNOLD FITNESS WEEKEND '96

Featuring...
★ The 8th Annual Schwarzenegger Classic
★ Ms International
★ Ms Fitness World
★ $300,000 In Prizes!
★ Arnold's Fitness EXPO '96 ...Hundreds of Exhibits!
★ Martial Arts Festival

The Body Building and Fitness Event of the Year!

FRIDAY, SATURDAY & SUNDAY, MARCH 1, 2, 3 1996 COLUMBUS, OHIO USA

Bottom-right window:

Forward | Home | Reload | Images | Open | Print | Find | Stop

`http://www.nytimes.com/bosnia/`

ew? | What's Cool? | Handbook | Net Search | Net Directory | Software

The New York Times
ON THE WEB

Bosnia: uncertain paths to peac

Continue into Bosnia: Uncertain Paths to Peace

To The New York Times on the Web

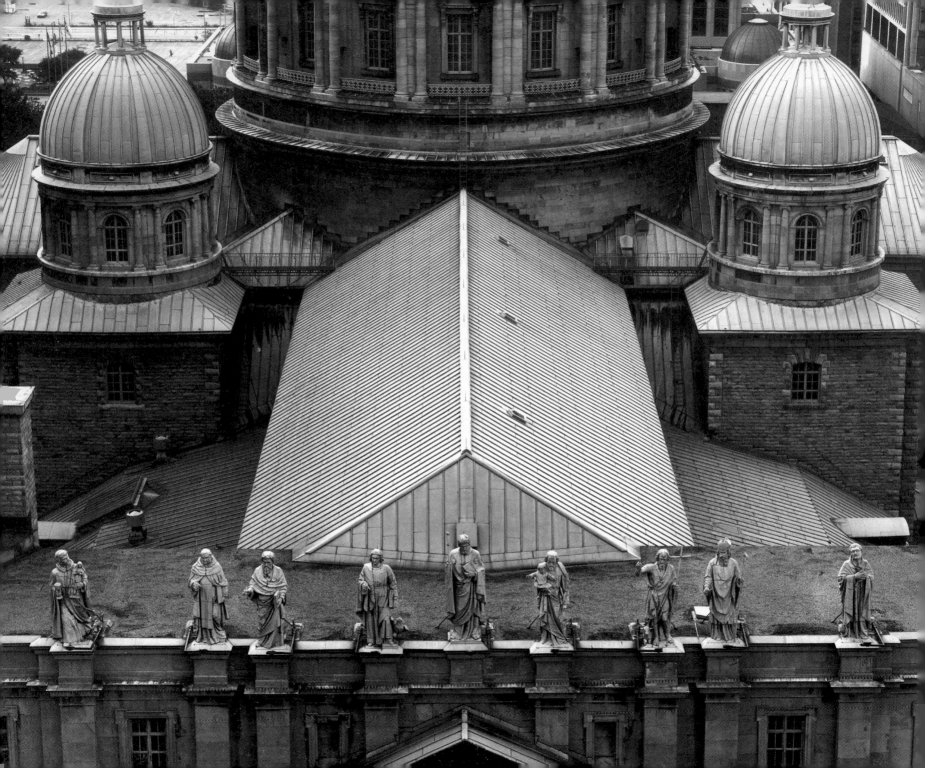

1937

The major event of McLuhan's life during his time at the University of Wisconsin was his conversion to Catholicism, which led him to look for employment in a Catholic university. In 1937, he was hired as an instructor in the English department of St. Louis University, a Jesuit school. From there, he conducted a courtship of Corinne Lewis, an actress from Fort Worth, Texas, whom he had met while doing research on his thesis at the Huntington Library in Pasadena, California.

Over the objections of Lewis's mother, a socially prominent, strong-willed, and staunchly Episcopalian matron who disliked McLuhan as a Catholic, a Yankee, and a man of dubious prospects (due to his poor pay as an academic), the couple married in 1939. The union was an enduring and largely happy one that produced six children; McLuhan, however, proved less than ideal as a father—he was preoccupied with his ideas, chronically impatient, and, at times, a stern disciplinarian.

Throughout the late thirties and forties, McLuhan chafed at his low pay and lack of recognition in the intellectual world. Although he published a number of articles in academic journals, they were a fraction of his prodigious output. Moreover, he was restless and dissatisfied with what he regarded as unsympathetic colleagues and mediocre students. ⊙

Cognitive Dissonance

McLuhan was what I would call a compartmentalized Roman Catholic. That is, he had a compartment in his head, sort of metaphorically, just like you might have a bulkhead on a ship to keep the compartments each sealed and contained so that if a torpedo hits one compartment, the entire ship won't sink and the other compartments won't flood. McLuhan, in my dealings with him over many years, kept his Catholicism separate in that way. He did not use a lot of theological scripture to substantiate his academic arguments. He did not appeal to religious nomenclature, for the most part, in an academic lesson. He sought to keep the two separate in a professional way, and also in a way that would keep him from experiencing cognitive dissonance. In the one quadrant of his brain, there were many elements he accepted on faith, but in the other quadrant there were elements for which he invited us to use skillful scholarly scrutiny to underpin their assumptions, and the two frequently don't mix. So I think of him as having a kind of apartheid in his apart-head, so to speak, between these two functions: one that required certain fundamental axioms that could not be challenged, and the other that was full of the probing, provoking, penetrating, constant reexamination of all academic assumptions, particularly those that he fought against—the structure and specialized forms and norms that he inherited and that he loved to debunk because he found them narrow-minded.

Tom Cooper

Left to right: Marshall and Corinne McLuhan set sail for their honeymoon in Europe, 1939; an armful of daughters: Mary, Teresa, Stephanie, and Elizabeth with their father in 1958; Marshall and Corinne on their tandem bicycle in the late seventies; Marshall and Corinne at home, 1973.

I am resolutely opposed to all innovation,

all change, but I am determined to understand what's happening. Because I don't choose just to sit and let the juggernaut roll over me. Many people seem to think that if you talk about something recent, you're in favor of it. The exact opposite is true in my case. Anything I talk about is almost certainly something I'm resolutely against. And it seems to me the best way to oppose it is to understand it. And then you know where to turn off the buttons.

Marshall McLuhan, *This Hour Has Seven Days*, CBC Television, 1966

Violence

Violence, whether spiritual or physical, is a quest for identity and the meaningful. The less identity, the more violence.

Marshall McLuhan, "Violence of the Media," *Canadian Forum,* 1976

and Identity

IT'S WHY THEY HAVE TO KILL

in order to find out whether they're real. This is where the violence comes from. This meaningless slaying around our streets is the work of people who have lost all identity and who have to kill in order to know if they're real or if the other guy's real. I suppose that one could even produce a theory of war to say that when a certain amount of technological change happens very quickly to a whole community, they are so lost about who they are that they want a basic war to find out. It's another way of crashing through to find one's identity. Violence as a form of quest for identity is one thing the people who have been ripped off feel the need of. He's going to show who he is, what his credentials are, that he's tough. So anybody on a psychic frontier tends to get tough or violent, and it's happening to us on a mass scale today. It might even be said that at the speed of light man has neither goals, objectives, nor private identity. He is an item in a data bank—software only, easily forgotten—and deeply resentful. Marshall McLuhan, "McLuhan probe," original source and date unknown

Above: The masses get the message: photo collage of Marshall McLuhan;
left to right: Marshall McLuhan in the seventies; McLuhan sought fame in a variety of ways,
including the *McLuhan Dew-Line,* a newsletter offering his insights; reading through
the news, 1972; McLuhan "probes" an interviewer in his University of Toronto office, 1968.

I'm sure McLuhan is coming back into fashion because the attention he gave to certain subjects is the same that we are giving those subjects today. He brought into focus areas of concern that have become not only pertinent, but urgent. We are taking another look at McLuhan, but it's not because people understand him any better. The number of people who understand McLuhan hasn't changed. Certainly not among the McLuhanites. Frankly, I think he's still difficult to understand. Understanding McLuhan is not a given. Certainly not any more now than it was in the sixties. **Derrick de Kerckhove**

Brain Bath

Sure, it's difficult to read McLuhan's work. You can read his work in many ways. You can read it as fragments. You can also try to read it whole, which is the enterprise I've been engaged in and that's marvelous—I mean it's like taking a brain bath. But in all of that, you can't make the mistake of forgetting that the very controversy McLuhan's ideas provoked fragmented his work forever. To understand McLuhan, you also have to understand all these fragments that show up nestling like little nuggets in people's texts, acknowledged or un-acknowledged in media commentary, in discussions, whenever we are trying to consider the effects of new media. The interesting thing about his relevance now is that in the wake of postmodernism, deconstructionism, and a whole series of intellectual movements, McLuhan no longer seems so eccentric.

Liss Jeffrey

Disincarnate

He was very complex. Most people did not understand him. In fact, I heard many people criticize his work who hadn't read much of it, and who hadn't comprehended what they'd read. He was not easy to get. He's a little easier now. When he talked about disincarnate existence, or the retribalizing effects of electric process, people just didn't get it. Now, we've caught up to the realities of electric culture. Now, when I talk to students and I say something about disincarnate reality after they've spent the morning surfing the Internet, they say, "Ho hum, so, yes, that's obvious." When I tell them that McLuhan was the author of that idea a long time ago, they become very excited about further exploring the work of someone who is making sense of the experiences they're having. **Frank Zingrone**

McLuhan had his supporters. However, they were few in number—a brave band. Most people greeted him with derision, probably out of jealousy. He made money, they didn't. He got fame, they didn't. He got attention, they didn't. They worked harder; he seemed to be playing all the time. He just had a grand time. But there is a misconception about that, too. He worked very hard. He never stopped. But he was playful in his work, and that was an important part of his philosophy. He used to say, "Without the play between the wheel and the axle, you have no movement. Everything seizes up." **Robert Logan**

1944

In 1944, McLuhan left St. Louis to join the faculty of Assumption College—now part of the University of Windsor—where he stayed for two years until he arrived at his permanent home, St. Michael's College at the University of Toronto. There, like other places he had taught, McLuhan found the students unsatisfactory and his colleagues often unsympathetic. The foremost English professor in the university at the time, A. S. P. Woodhouse, detested the New Criticism, the Catholic Church, and Marshall McLuhan personally. Throughout McLuhan's career, a large percentage of his colleagues at the university regarded him as academically unsound—he rarely substantiated his arguments and was cavalier about facts. Moreover, as McLuhan himself admitted, he was a poor listener and often carried on monologues rather than genuine conversations. ☉

What is very little understood about the electronic age is that it angelizes man, disembodies him. Turns him into software.

Marshall McLuhan, *Marshall McLuhan with A. F. Knowles,* York University Instructional Services Video, 1971

He was like the fastest gun in the West. People wanted to top his verbal repertoire, his wit, his turnaround of phrases, his verbal acrobatics, his command of literature. And so he loved a good sparring partner who could keep a ninety-mile-per-hour brain going against his. He often challenged his students to see their own pedantry, their own conventional wisdom, their own mediocrity of thinking, and often he'd return papers saying, "One idea" or "Two ideas" at the top, with no other comment. In other words, he was only interested in good new ideas. **Tom Cooper**

Mass Audience

Any medium presents a figure whose ground is always hidden or subliminal. In the case of TV, as of the telephone and radio, the subliminal ground could be called the disincarnate or disembodied user. This is to say that when you are "on the telephone" or "on the air," you do not have a physical body. In these media, the sender is sent and is instantaneously present everywhere. The disembodied user extends to all those who are recipients of electric information. It is these people who constitute the mass audience, because mass is a factor of speed rather than quantity, although popular speech permits the term mass to be used with large publics.

Marshall McLuhan, "A Last Look at the Tube," *New York* magazine, 1978

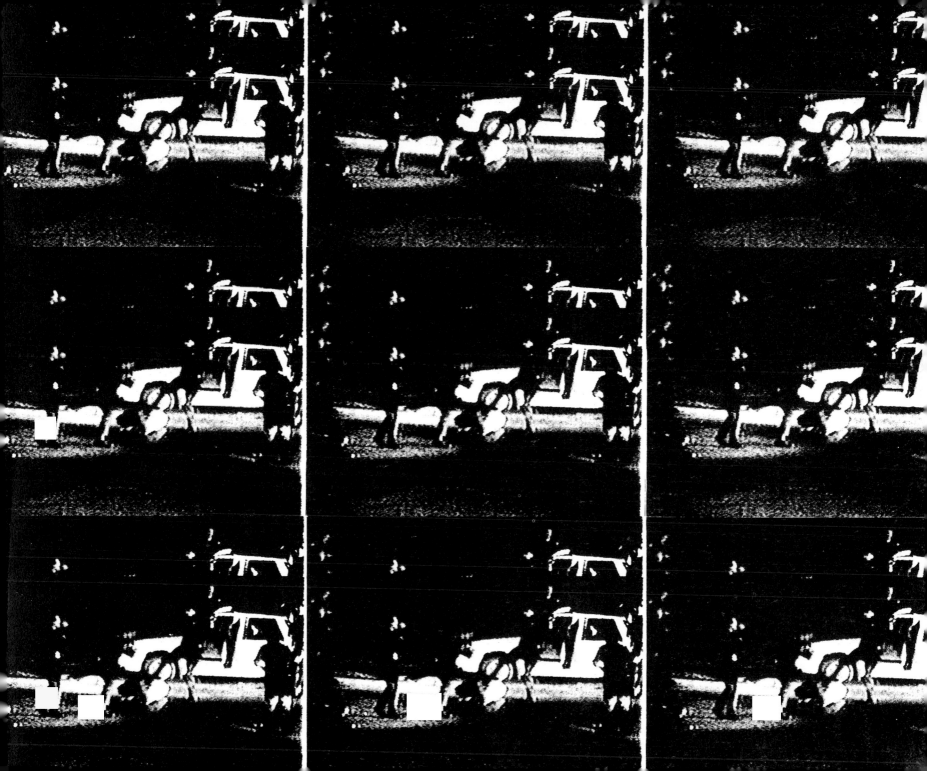

I'm a McLuhan skeptic for probably a silly reason. I had a bizarre encounter over the telephone with him when I was a junior editor at the Toronto *Globe and Mail* and he had written a piece that I didn't understand—the first sentence right up to the last sentence. But I knew my duty, and I had to phone him for some clarifications that a senior editor had asked for, and I read the clarifications to him and all I could remember him saying was, "McLuhan wouldn't have said that, McLuhan would have said this." I realized that anyone who talks about themselves in the third-person singular has slightly lost it. But I realized that I was talking to the guru of the age so I humbly hung up the phone.

John Fraser

The violence that all electric media inflict on their users is that they are instantly invaded and deprived of their physical bodies and are merged in a network of extensions of their own nervous systems. As if this were not sufficient violence or invasion of individual rights, the elimination of the physical bodies of the electric media users also deprives them of the means of relating the program experience of their private, individual selves, even as instant involvement suppresses private identity.

The loss of individual and personal meaning via the electronic media ensures a corresponding and reciprocal violence from those so deprived of their identities; for violence, whether spiritual or physical, is a quest for identity and the meaningful. The less identity, the more violence. Marshall McLuhan, "Violence of the Media," *Canadian Forum,* 1976

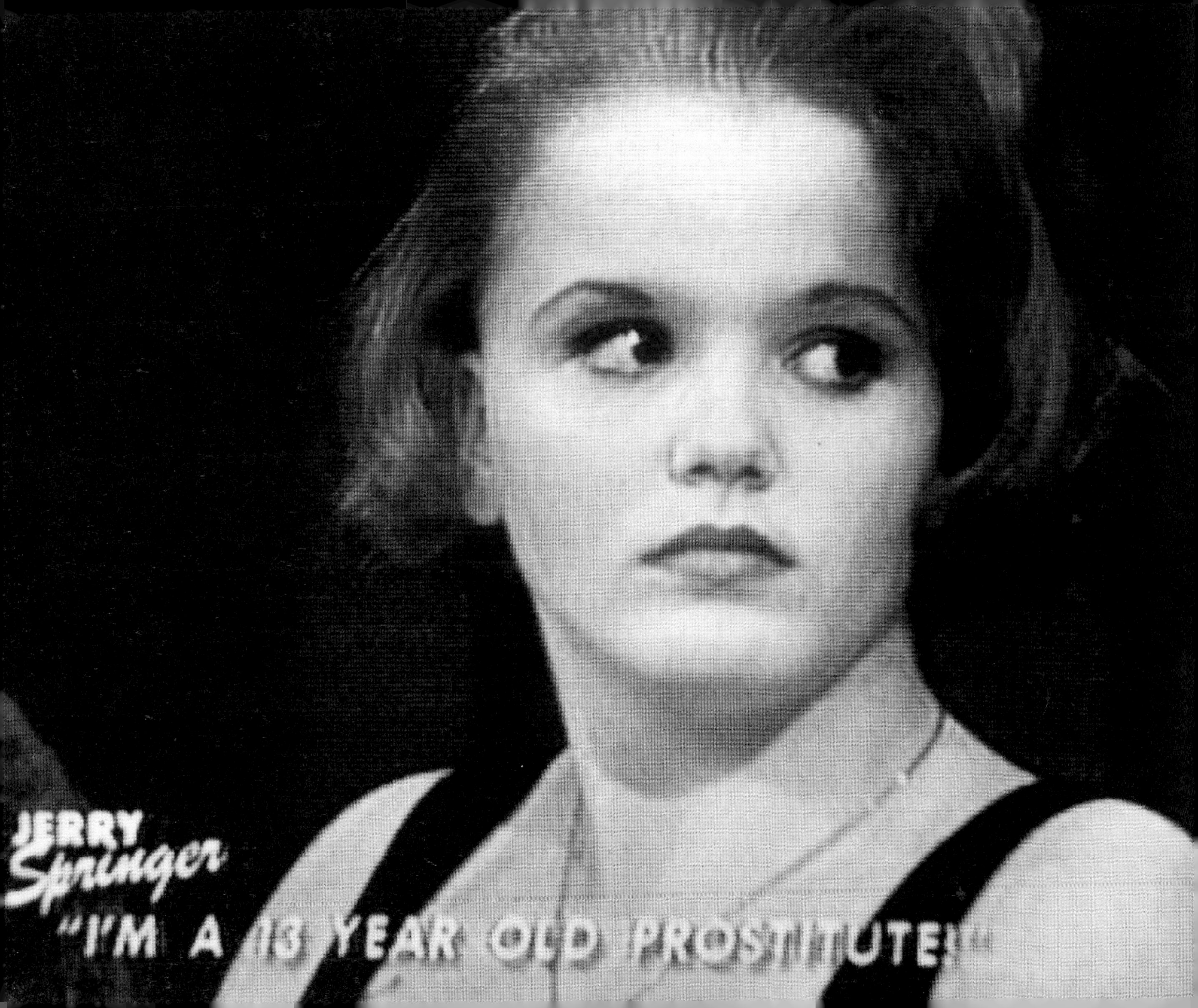
JERRY
Springer
"I'M A 13 YEAR OLD PROSTITUTE!"

SUPERMAN

The electric surround of information that has tended to make man a superman at the same time reduces him into a pretty pitiable nobody by merging him with everybody. It has extended man in a colossal, superhuman way, but it has not made individuals feel important. Our astronauts were real skyscrapers but they don't seem or feel very important as private persons. Electrically, the corporate human scale has become vast even as private identity shrinks to the pitiable. The ordinary man can feel so pitiably weak that, like a skyjacker, he'll reach for a superhuman dimension of world coverage in a wild, desperate effort for fulfillment, or he will buy a private psychiatrist to be an audience. Violence on a colossal scale results from his feeling of impotence. The media tend to make everybody puny, while offering them the opportunity to be supermen. So there is a new desire to use the media to put on the colossal audience that today's media provide.

Marshall McLuhan, "Making Contact with Marshall McLuhan," interview by Louis Forsdale, 1974

The psychiatrist's couches of the world are sagging with people who have lost their sense of identity. They used to feel they were clearly defined entities; they had cards of identity, they knew who they were. Now they go to psychiatrists to be told or to find out, "Who am I? What should I be doing?" Marshall McLuhan, *Take Thirty*, CBC Television, 1965

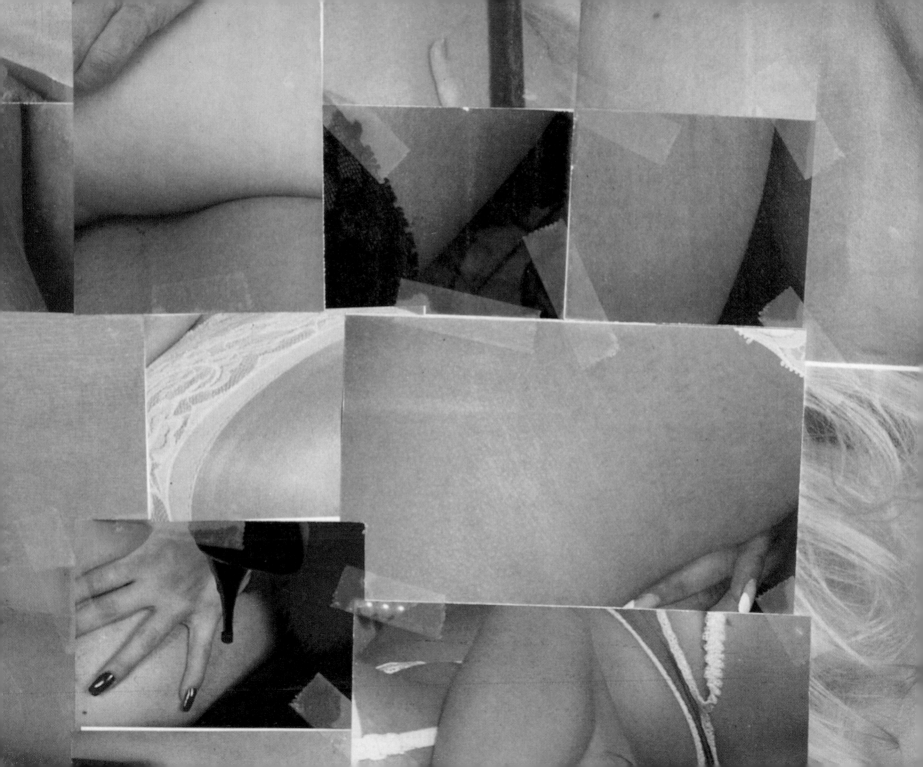

Sensations And Kicks

Pornography and obscenity . . . work by specialism and fragmentation. They deal with figure without a ground — situations in which the human factor is suppressed in favor of sensations and kicks. In the same way, the individual can be separated out from the society, Robinson Crusoe–style. I first began to explain . . . that pornography and violence are by-products of societies in which private identity has been scrubbed or destroyed by sudden environmental change, or unexpected confrontations that disrupt the image the individual or the group entertains of itself. Any loss of identity prompts people to seek reassurance and rediscovery of themselves by testing, and even by violence. Today, the electric revolution, the wired planet, and the information environment involve everybody in everybody to the point of individual extinction. Marshall McLuhan, letter to Clare Westcott, 1975

1963

McLuhan found important allies among the faculty at the University of Toronto, chiefly a fellow English professor named Claude Bissell, who later became president of the university. In 1963, Bissell backed McLuhan when he sought, successfully, to establish the Centre for Culture and Technology—a kind of one-man think tank under his directorship. McLuhan, while antagonizing from time to time some of the Basilian priests who ran St. Michael's College, also found enough sympathy there that he was basically left alone. As for his students, many of them loved McLuhan for the wit and intellectual stimulation he provided, but others were disturbed because he was more interested in talking about his ideas than the subjects on his course outlines. ⊙

McLuhan at King's College Circle, University of Toronto, 1969.

How did I meet him? I simply wandered into a University of Toronto English class at St. Michael's College, where he was giving a guest lecture. I wasn't expecting much because up until then I wasn't being excited intellectually. But the experience of McLuhan's lecture was so remarkable that I found I had cold sweat trickling down my sides. I was so excited! I can hardly explain to you how wonderful it was to have the twentieth century suddenly explained and dropped onto my plate like a possibility that would never end. I remember when the lecture (which was on the contemporary significance of the French Symbolist poets) was over, I was in this state of exalted completion and a guy studying for the priesthood who had been sitting beside me got up and said, "Wow, he was really out in left field today. Did you get any of that?" And we left the hall together, then parted ways. **Frank Zingrone**

The Hunter

Quest for identity, quest for food, quest for anything, quest for awareness. Researchers, CIA, a whole bunch of hunters. All the business community, all the learned community is engaged in hunting today. We don't have goals anymore; we play the total field. The hunter plays the field. He doesn't have a goal anymore. These are the images of our time—the hunter. All the key figures of our time are hunters. Hunting is pure thrill. Knowledge-seeking is pure thrill. Marshall McLuhan, *Ideas,* CBC Radio, 1969

He threw out these paragraphs, probes, bits and pieces. His whole life was like a seminar with a brilliant professor who sits there surrounded by students throwing out this idea and that idea. Some of the students go off and write a wonderful paper based on one of those ideas, another one goes off and maybe writes a masterpiece based on it. Another one doesn't get anything, doesn't understand what the professor is talking about, thinks he is erratic and crazy. That's what McLuhan was.

In the 1990s, a number of people have rediscovered him, I think, because a number of the things he said, which where not quite so true when he said them, are much more true now. I would say that CNN is something that all of us look at from time to time and most of us think about from time to time. It was born the year McLuhan died — 1980. Anyway, people look at CNN and they realize they are watching something live in Tiananmen Square; they are watching the Berlin Wall fall; they are watching these things as they are happening and the term that McLuhan popularized — global village — has a great meaning for people today. They can understand it in their own lives. And so people are looking back at his work to see what he was saying and what insights he might have for the life of our time with its computers and very different kinds of communication.

Robert Fulford

MILITARY SKILL

MILITARY SKILL

MILITARY SKIL

CAMOUFLAGE

PHONETIC ALPHABET

NIGHT VISION GOGGLES

COURTES

LEADER

LEADER

MILITARY ASSET
Missile

GENERAL H. NORMAN
SCHWARZKOPF

SADDAM HUSSEIN

MIM-104 PATRIOT

GENERAL COLIN POWELL

Canadians are all a very humble bunch. They take it for granted that everything they do must be second-rate.

Marshall McLuhan, "Conversations with Marshall McLuhan," interview by G. E. Stearn, *Encounter*, 1967

McLuhan's character was distinctly Canadian, although he often railed against what he considered Canadian timidity and small-mindedness. The Victorian age lingered on the Canadian prairies where McLuhan grew up, and he never lost a sense of high purpose, a strenuous innocence characteristic of that time and place. More importantly, he reveled in the freedom of being Canadian—in the positive aspect of the country's weak national identity. No heavy burdens of history, no compelling national myths stood in the way of his perceiving the world. While many Canadians complained about excessive American influence affecting the country, he liked to say that Canadians enjoyed complete access to American experience with no commitment to American goals. ⊙

He wrote about Canada and was concerned about Canada. I don't think he had the slightest personal gain in mind when he went to meet with [Prime Minister] Pierre Trudeau. He was going straight for the jugular. He went to the guy who had the most to say for the country; he wanted to see him succeed. McLuhan was concerned about Canada so he spoke to the head of the country. Trudeau also happened to be a very intelligent man so that made the conversation easier and more exciting. That is the way McLuhan related to the prime minister. He was never proud of himself because he was talking to the head of the nation. **Derrick de Kerckhove**

The Americans have lost their sense of identity. The country is falling apart physically and politically because of the speed of information. The American bureaucracy, political and educational, was set up for very slow speeds of the printed word and railways. At electric speeds, nothing in the U.S.A. makes sense.

Marshall McLuhan, *The New Majority with Ed Fitzgerald*, CBC Television, 1970

Marshall and Corinne enjoy the afternoon sailing the Aegean with friends in September 1963.

1951

In 1951, McLuhan published his first book, The Mechanical Bride: Folklore of Industrial Man. *It had been long in the making—since his days at the University of Wisconsin, in the late thirties. For years, he had been gathering magazine advertisements and writing essays about them, analyzing not only their rhetorical strategies but the underlying social attitudes they conveyed. It was a form of social criticism partly inspired by his old Cambridge professor, F. R. Leavis, whose* Culture and Environment, *published in 1933, had urged literary intellectuals to study radio broadcasts, advertisements, and popular journalism in an effort to combat their inherent philistinism.*

The title of McLuhan's book reflected his belief that industrial technology had, in effect, mechanized human life and the means of production. In this respect, the book also owed a great deal to the Swiss architect Sigfried Giedion, whose book, Mechanization Takes Command *(1948), demonstrated how everything from nineteenth-century bathroom fixtures to Marcel Duchamps's painting* Nude Descending a Staircase *showed the influence of mechanization. McLuhan resented what he considered industrialism's baneful effect on family life—emasculating fathers who no longer practiced time-honored crafts but worked under humiliating circumstances in offices and factories; domineering women; and increased homosexuality. His favorite cultural symbol of this state of affairs was the comic strip hero Dagwood Bumstead, who was berated by his wife, Blondie, and casually despised by his children.* ⊙

Echo

In the eighties, as we transfer our whole being to the data bank, privacy will become a ghost or echo of its former self and what remains of community will disappear.

Marshall McLuhan, "Living at the Speed of Light," *Maclean's* magazine, 1980

McLuhan's first book, *The Mechanical Bride*, 1951.

I think his understanding of the nature of the media is now making itself clear to a lot of people coming at it from a lot of different angles. Also, his writing tends to be very oracular and prophetic and filled with metaphor, and allows many interpretations. It's not a rigid setting forth of doctrine so it's possible to take McLuhan's writing and develop it in a lot of different directions. It provides seeds for strands of theory that sprout. Also, a lot of what he said is now much more obvious; we have fiber optics, we have MTV, we have technology that didn't exist, so people are now seeing the effects of that technology. His phrase "the global village," for example, is much more apparent after one has been exposed to CNN or the Internet than it was when neither of those technologies existed. **Lewis Lapham**

Fantasy Violence

The fantasy violence on TV is a reminder that the violence of the real world is much motivated by people questing for lost identity. Rollo May and others have pointed out that violence in the real world is the mark of those questing for identity. On the frontier, everybody is a nobody, and therefore, the frontier manifests the patterns of toughness and vigorous action on the part of those trying to find out who they are.

Marshall McLuhan, "A Last Look at the Tube," *New York* magazine, 1978

Violence — in the sense of crossing boundaries and seeking new identities, and just the general quest for knowledge and identity — is the way we live. The tragic hero constantly renewing the human image is a violent man.

Marshall McLuhan, *The New Majority with Ed Fitzgerald*, CBC Television, 1970

Electronic Man

Everybody at a football game is a nobody simply by virtue of the fact of their deep involvement in an experience simultaneously shared by many others. In such a situation, the most famous person in the world becomes a nobody. This is a structural fact, and when considered in relation to our wired planet, where everybody is involved in everybody's experience, this is the overwhelming backlash of reduction to nonentity — the creation of mass man. The mass man is not the vulgar or the stupid or the unthinking man, but anybody and everybody who experiences the electric situation of instant information.

Electronic man is no abstraction, but rather the existing individual in a simultaneous culture. Having had his private individuality erased anonymously, he is paranoiac and much inclined to violence, for violence is a quest for identity, seeking to discover, "Who am I?" and "What are my limits?"

Marshall McLuhan, speech at the Conference on Management Information Systems, 1971

I think a great deal of the confusion and misery of our time is related to the fact that people are still trying to find goals in a world that is moving so fast that no possible goal could remain in focus for ten seconds.

Marshall McLuhan, *Telescope Revisited,* CBC Television, 1967

When things come at you very fast,

naturally you lose touch with yourself. Anybody moving into a new world loses identity. If you go to China, and you've never been there before, you're a nobody. You can't relate to anything there. So loss of identity is something that happens in rapid change. But everybody at the speed of light tends to become a nobody. This is what's called the masked man. The masked man has no identity. He is so deeply involved in other people that he doesn't have any personal identity.

Marshall McLuhan, "McLuhan probe," original source and date unknown

Everybody at the speed of light tends to become a nobody.

Marshall McLuhan, "McLuhan probe," original source and date unknown

Medium is

The telephone: speech without walls.
The phonograph: music hall without walls.
The photograph: museum without walls.
The electric light: space without walls.
The movie, radio, and TV: classroom without walls.

Marshall McLuhan, *Understanding Media*, 1964

the Message

THE CLOCK DRAGGED MAN OUT OF THE WORLD

of seasonal rhythms and recurrence as effectively as the alphabet had released him from the magical resonance of the spoken word and the tribal trap. This dual translation of the individual out of the grip of nature and out of the clutch of the tribe was not without its own penalties. But the return to nature and the return to the tribe are, under electric conditions, fatally simple. We need beware of those who announce programs for restoring man to the original state and language of the race. These crusaders have never examined the role of media and technology in tossing man about from dimension to dimension. Marshall McLuhan, *Understanding Media*, 1964

1958 As the fifties wore on, McLuhan began to find more and more audiences receptive to his explorations, although most remained skeptical about his actual conclusions. In 1959, the National Association of Educational Broadcasters (NAEB) in the United States asked McLuhan to develop a syllabus for the study of media in schools—a project that became the nucleus of his most famous work, Understanding Media: The Extensions of Man. It was during an address at a 1958 convention of the NAEB that McLuhan first uttered, in a highly public forum, his famous phrase "the medium is the message"—meaning, among other things, that all media have effects on the human psyche quite apart from the explicit bits of information they might convey. Eventually, he became famous for this slogan, as well as the phrase "global village," which he coined as a description of the new world of electronic broadcasting. ⊙

On page 167 of *The Greening of America*, Charles Reich notes that "the medium is the message means that there is no content in any medium." This statement is actually one of the few useful remarks that has ever come to my attention about anything I have written. It enables me to see that the user of the electric light—or a hammer, or a language, or a book—is the content. As such, there is a total metamorphosis of the user by the interface. It is the metamorphosis that I consider the message.

Marshall McLuhan, letter to Edward T. Hall, 1971

Total Situation

The new electric structuring and configuring of life more and more encounters the old lineal and fragmentary procedures and tools of analysis from the mechanical age. More and more we turn from the content of messages to study total effect. Kenneth Boulding put this matter in *The Image* by saying, "The meaning of a message is the change that it produces in the image." Concern with effect rather than meaning is a basic change of our electric time, for effect involves the total situation and not a single level of information movement.

Marshall McLuhan, *Understanding Media*, 1964

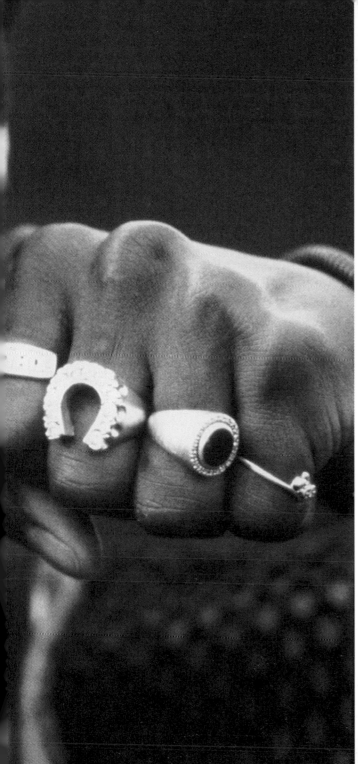

Sontag, Fabio, Warhol, & Oldenburg

I consider McLuhan a great personal role model for me because he was a professor, a very learned man who was suddenly caught in the public spotlight. Suddenly, he was in this magazine and that magazine. He was taken up by journalists. People would call him up and ask him questions on all kinds of topics, from the simple to the abstruse. We haven't had anyone like that—before me—since McLuhan. He was the harbinger of a whole new kind of fusion of academe and media. I have always said that there is too big a gap in America between the world of scholarship and the world of mass media in which people live, in which everything gets done.

I feel that it's a function of the intellectual in America to close that gap. I feel that Susan Sontag started to do it and then pulled back and became very snobbish and began chasing all kinds of French intellectuals, foreign intellectuals—who became more interesting to her than our own mass media. For me, Marshall McLuhan's experience—and I think that the speed at which I became a kind of pop figure—shows that there is a vacuum. It is a vacuum waiting to be filled. The speed at which I began to be the subject of cartoons, with which suddenly journalists enjoyed quoting me on some topic—and I'm quoted on everything from Fabio, to, like, the most recent penis-cutting incident in Virginia—is wonderful. McLuhan created the persona of the scholar who was also the cultural commentator, who reconciles in his own mind, in his own person, the terrible division we have between high culture and popular culture.

Despite everything that the great pop artists Andy Warhol and Claes Oldenburg did, we still have a terrible gap. Rock and roll, to me one of the great art forms of the end of the century, still has never gained the respect it deserves from critics. There are people who are rock fans and have written serious books about it, but people who are untouched by rock music have absolutely no respect for it. There's still a lot of work to be done following in the steps of McLuhan. **Camille Paglia**

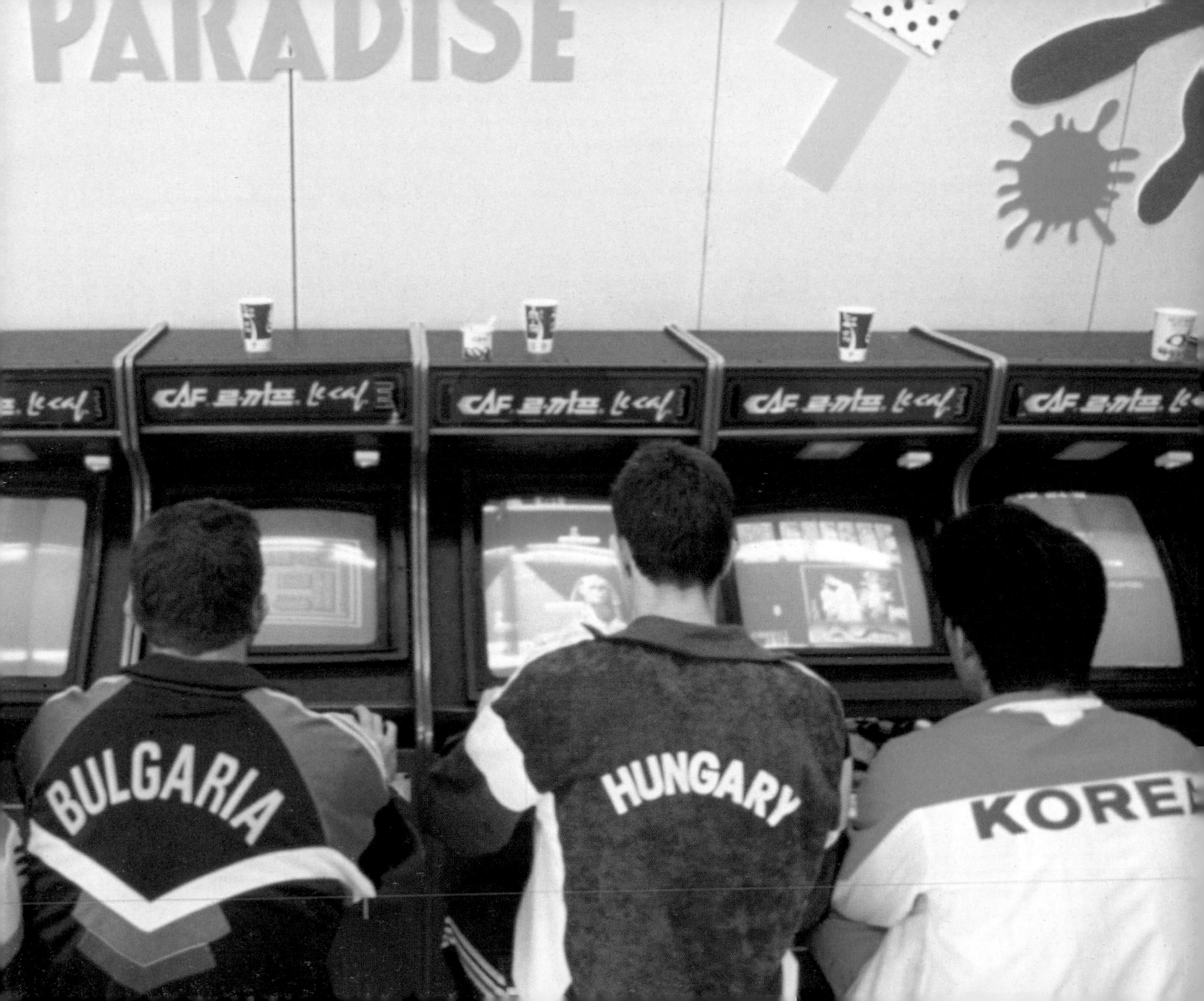
PARADISE
BULGARIA
HUNGARY
KORE

Humpty-Dumpty

Print was a great improvement on the older alphabetic writing. Print is not only a technology of movable types and of the first mechanization of a handicraft, it had all of the startling implications that automation now has for us with regard to the reorganizing of work. Print reorganized the work pattern by specialism. Instead of a man knowing all aspects of his craft, he learned one operation only and work was broken up into bits. Humpty-Dumpty literally fell off the wall with print, and the types were scattered hither and thither. But print created a new environment. Any technology creates a new environment, a new set of relationships among people. Print created the public; no kind of handwriting was capable of creating a public. It wasn't strong enough or powerful enough technologically to create what is called a public. With print came into existence for the first time in human history the public. Marshall McLuhan, *Take Thirty,* CBC Television, 1965

Only the phonetic alphabet makes a break between eye and ear, between semantic meaning and visual code, and thus, only phonetic writing has the power to translate man from the tribal to the civilized sphere, to give him an eye for an ear.

Marshall McLuhan, *The Gutenberg Galaxy*, 1962

1962 McLuhan's fame exploded in the sixties. The process began in 1962 with the publication of The Gutenberg Galaxy: The Making of Typographic Man, *a study of the revolution in sensibility wrought by the printing press; and, in 1964, of* Understanding Media: The Extensions of Man, *a look at various media, including money, clothing, and cars, as well as print and television. Both books caught the attention of critics and intellectuals in North America and Europe.* ⊙

McLuhan displays *Understanding Media*.

He wrote The Gutenberg Galaxy at the old library at St. Michael's College [at the University of Toronto]. He had the books of people he had read or heard about open at the appropriate pages and a couple seminarians running from one book to another taking quotes down, and he would string them together with blurbs or commentaries of his own. That was the way McLuhan wrote *The Gutenberg Galaxy*. And he was reproached for his method. People said he was plagiarizing or ripping off other people's ideas. He didn't see it that way at all. He saw that by using these chunks — these gems, these fragments that you shore up against your ruins, as T.S. Eliot would say — in a new way, he would actually give them a different content and meaning. **Derrick de Kerckhove**

The Greek myth about the alphabet was that Cadmus, reputedly the king who introduced phonetic letters into Greece, sowed the dragon's teeth and they sprang up armed men. Like any other myth, this one capsulates a prolonged process into a flashing insight. The alphabet meant power and authority and control of military structures at a distance. When combined with papyrus, the alphabet spelled the end of the stationary temple bureaucracies and the priestly monopolies of knowledge and power. Unlike pre-alphabetic writing, which with its innumerable signs was difficult to master, the alphabet could be learned in a few hours. The acquisition of so extensive a knowledge and so complex a skill as pre-alphabetic writing, when applied to such unwieldy materials as brick and stone, ensured for the scribal caste a monopoly of priestly power. The easier alphabet and the light, cheap, transportable papyrus together effected the transfer of power from the priestly to the military class. All this is implied in the myth about Cadmus and the dragon's teeth, including the fall of the city-states, the rise of empires, and military bureaucracies.

Marshall McLuhan, *Understanding Media*, 1964

I think what people recognized intuitively but did not put a name on was the fact that Marshall was not an analyst, not a historian, not a sociologist, but a poet. What he was delivering to the world was a set of metaphors that we had to wrestle with, that worked at the essential metaphoric level of poetry, meaning he'd had a vision of the way in which the natural order of words supports a new perception of something. His focus was on literature, first, and then the broader aspects of communication. He was just loading us with these tremendously vivid verbal insights and we had to wrestle with them. People loved it. The stuff came to its apex in the sixties, when there was a new appetite for tolerance—respect for the poetic mode right across the whole fabric of society—and everybody just swallowed it up. It was wonderful. We played back his phrases as if we knew what they meant. **Patrick Watson**

The photographer being photographed: McLuhan behind the lens, date unknown.

Visual Bias

The printing press was the ultimate extension of phonetic literacy. Books could be reproduced in infinite numbers; universal literacy was at last fully possible, if gradually realized; and books became portable individual possessions. Type, the prototype of all machines, ensured the primacy of the visual bias and finally sealed the doom of tribal man. The new medium of linear, uniform, repeatable type produced information in unlimited quantities and at hitherto impossible speeds, thus assuring the eye a position of total predominance in man's sensorium. As a drastic extension of man, it shaped and transformed his entire environment, psychic and social, and was directly responsible for the rise of such disparate phenomena as nationalism, the Reformation, the assembly line, and its offspring, the Industrial Revolution. Marshall McLuhan, "Playboy Interview: Marshall McLuhan," interview by Eric Norden, *Playboy,* 1969

COMITÉ PROVENÇAL
PRÉSIDENT
COMITÉ PROVENÇAL
PRÉSIDENT
COMITÉ PROVENÇAL
PRÉSIDENT
Exigez avec le Front National
référendum
LAJOINIE au 1er tour LE VOTE à GAUCHE
LAJOINIE au 1er tour LE VOTE à GAUCHE
Quelle que soit votre intention au second tour
Au 1er tour
PETITS BOULOTS, FRIC-FACS, RACISME...
NOUS, ON DIT: ASSEZ!
LE 24 AVRIL ON VOTERA LAJOINIE.
LAJOINIE
Parti Communiste
26 MARS 1988
TOUS A AIX avec le
Ils attaquent la sécu
LA SYMBOLIQUE DES CATHEDRALES
Face aux politiques d'austérité, de regression sociale, d'atteintes aux libertés, de surarmement
exigeons!
LAJOINIE
au 1er tour

The phonetic alphabet and the printed word that exploded
the closed tribal world into the open society of fragmented functions and specialist knowledge and action
have never been studied in their roles as a magical
transformer. The antithetic electric power of instant
information that reverses social explosion into implosion,
private enterprise into organization man, and expanding
empires into common markets has obtained as little
recognition as the written word. The power of radio to
retribalize mankind, its almost instant reversal of indi-
vidualism into collectivism, fascist or Marxist, has gone
unnoticed. So extraordinary is this unawareness that *it*
is what needs to be explained. The transforming power
of media is easy to explain, but the ignoring of this
power is not at all easy to explain. It goes without saying that the universal ignoring of the psychic action
of technology bespeaks some inherent function, some
essential numbing of consciousness such as occurs
under stress and shock conditions.

Marshall McLuhan, *Understanding Media,* 1964

Teaching Machine

The book was the first teaching machine and also the first mass-produced commodity. In amplifying and extending the written word, typography revealed and greatly extended the structure of writing. Today, with the cinema and the electric speed-up of information movement, the formal structure of the printed word, as of mechanism in general, stands forth like a branch washed up on the beach. A new medium is never an addition to an old one, nor does it leave the old one in peace. It never ceases to oppress the older media until it finds new shapes and positions for them. Manuscript culture had sustained an oral procedure in education that was called Scholasticism at its higher levels; but by putting the same text in front of any given number of students or readers, print ended the scholastic regime of oral disputation very quickly. Print provided a vast new memory for past writings that made a personal memory inadequate. Marshall McLuhan, *Understanding Media,* 1964

I would say from roughly 1956 until he died, I took every opportunity I could to listen to him speak and to have conversations with him—although the word conversation has to be explained. I don't think I ever really did have a conversation with McLuhan and I don't recall being present when anyone else actually had a conversation. Mostly, you listened, let him play out this tape that he had in his mind. And it was always fascinating. Even when you asked him questions, you had the feeling that although he always seemed to be answering your question, he was just going on with the tape. No one I knew ever really resented that; we considered it a privilege to be present so we could listen and watch the tape unwind itself. **Neil Postman**

1960 *The spirit of the time was receptive to the all-embracing and basically optimistic theory of change that McLuhan offered. Events as varied as the Second Vatican Council and the election of John F. Kennedy signaled the onset of a bracing mood of adventure in the Western world, a promise of old certainties crumbling and new worlds in the making. The war in Vietnam soured the atmosphere but hastened the breakdown of social conventions. The sexual revolution, the hippie phenomena, campus riots, the widespread use of marijuana and LSD and other psychotropic drugs—everything seemed to point to an apocalyptic break with the past.*

Throughout the sixties, McLuhan explained it all, while he continued as an English professor at the University of Toronto, teaching courses, conducting seminars at his new Centre for Culture and Technology, arguing with his colleagues in the faculty lunchroom. ⊙

Media Fallout

Education is ideally civil defense against media fallout. Yet Western man has had, so far, no education or equipment for meeting any of the new media on their own terms. Literate man is not only numb and vague in the presence of film or photo, but he intensifies his ineptness by a defensive arrogance and condescension to "pop kulch" and "mass entertainment." It was in this spirit of bulldog opacity that the Scholastic philosophers failed to meet the challenge of the printed book in the sixteenth century. The vested interests of acquired knowledge and conventional wisdom have always been bypassed and engulfed by new media.

Marshall McLuhan, *Understanding Media,* 1964

McLuhan's Centre for Culture and Technology at the University of Toronto was a converted coach house where he ran his famous "Monday night sessions." Guests ranged from students to then Prime Minister Pierre Trudeau.

Education, which should be helping youth to understand and adapt to their revolutionary new environments, is instead being used merely as an instrument of cultural aggression, imposing upon retribalized youth the obsolescent visual values of the dying literate age. Our entire educational system is reactionary, oriented to past values and past technologies, and will likely continue so until the old generation relinquishes power. The generation gap is actually a chasm, separating not two age-groups but two vastly divergent cultures. I can understand the ferment in our schools because our educational system is totally rearview mirror. It's a dying and outdated system founded on literate values and fragmented and classified data totally unsuited to the needs of the first television generation.

Marshall McLuhan, "Playboy Interview: Marshall McLuhan," interview by Eric Norden, *Playboy*, 1969

Trojan Horse

I would suggest that if you were to put the TV in the classroom, it would blow the classroom to bits. The teaching processes would be completely transformed: it would be exactly like bringing the Trojan horse inside the walls of Troy. It would not be an incidental teaching aid, it would simply alter the entire pattern and procedures of the classroom and create an altogether new educational form. However, this has, in effect, happened since TV is already the environmental force that is shaping the awareness and outlook of children everywhere. It is already doing this anyway, so whether it goes into the classroom or not is really not a great issue.

Marshall McLuhan, *Take Thirty*, CBC Television, 1965

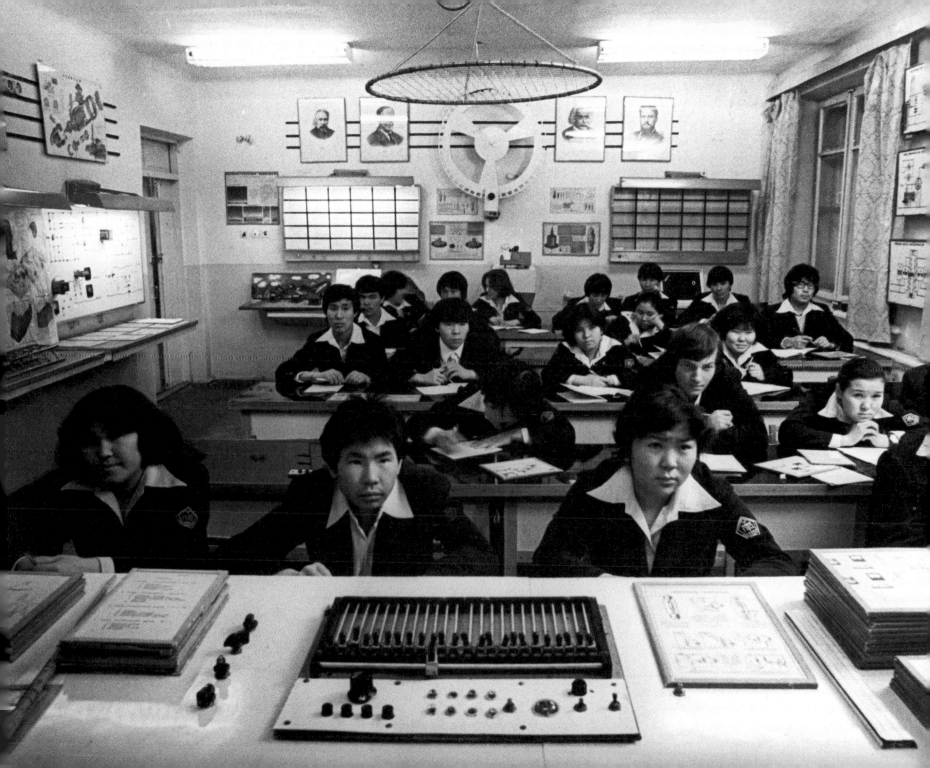

When you say the medium is the message, you're uttering an obvious contradiction, because we normally reserve the word "message" for the content and "medium" for the container, as it were. So the first reaction to the contradiction or paradox ought to be to examine the terms a little more closely.

Suppose it were a poem, a haiku, "The Medium is the Message" run out to seventeen syllables. Were it cast that way you'd immediately rush to the dictionary to check if what the speaker or writer meant is what you thought. In fact, it doesn't mean what appears on the surface, and the trouble with it comes from most people's not delving below the surface. My father was usually quite exact when he made statements like that, statements intended to provoke attention and thought. He may have had tongue in cheek and twinkle in eye, but he was being quite precise.

If you say the medium is the message you're talking about a medium meaning a milieu—medium in the sense of growing medium for plants, for example. A medium is an entire circumstance or situation that makes something else burgeon forth or appear. To say that that is the message of a technology ... well, now, that brings out a completely different dimension. That is to say that every innovation, every new gadget like a pocket calculator or coffee cup or TV camera, brings with it a whole environment or milieu of not just *assumptions* but ways of thinking, ways of feeling, ways of organizing your life—a whole range of services and disservices without which the item would not function. Like electricity, without which I couldn't be part of this interview: it is needed for the lights, the cameras, to power the equipment. Electricity is part of the medium of TV and is therefore part of the message of the camera or the light bulb or the TV set. Electricity has meant quite a lot of reorganization in our lives: that is the message, and the "massage" we get from it. **Eric McLuhan**

Manuscript notes: McLuhan's thoughts on effects of the media

Proj~~ect~~ McLuhan

⚡ To foster the ~~broadest~~ discussion immarginable
That the TV image is in effect a massive
Bauhaus program.

That the TV image is haptic rather than photographically
visual.
That the TV viewer is engaged in skin-diving.

That the TV image, like any technological extension of our sensorium, has the power
to alter the existing ratio among our
senses, and thus to alter sensibility and even
mental processes.
That the medium is the message.
That the program "content" of any medium
is another medium, as speech is the "content" of
                                                phonetic writing.
That the content of a medium like the
"meaning" of a poem is   the juicy piece
of meat carried by the burglar to distract
the housedog of the mind, and thus to let
the poem do its work

That media are "hot" when their images are
of "high definition" or when charged with data, as
with print rather than manuscript, or radio
rather than telephone, or film rather
than TV.
That hot media are consumer-oriented and
cool media are producer-oriented.

Electric light is pure information. It is a medium without a message, as it were, unless it is used to spell out some verbal ad or name. This fact, characteristic of all media, means that the content of any medium is always another medium. The content of writing is speech, just as the written word is the content of print and print is the content of the telegraph. If it is asked, "What is the content of speech?" it is necessary to say, "It is an actual process of thought, which is in itself nonverbal."

Marshall McLuhan, *Understanding Media*, 1964

Clear Vision

Indeed, it is only too typical that the content of any medium blinds us to the character of the medium. It is only today that industries have become aware of the various kinds of business in which they are engaged. When IBM discovered that it was not in the business of making office equipment or business machines, but that it was in the business of processing information, then it began to navigate with clear vision. The General Electric Company makes a considerable portion of its profits from electric light bulbs and lighting systems. It has not yet discovered that, quite as much as AT&T, it is in the business of moving information. Marshall McLuhan, *Understanding Media*, 1964

Watchdog Of The Mind

I am in the position of Louis Pasteur telling doctors that their greatest enemy was quite invisible and quite unrecognized by them. Our conventional response to all media — namely, that it is how they are used that counts — is the numb stance of the technological idiot. For the content of a medium is like the juicy piece of meat carried by the burglar to distract the watchdog of the mind. The effect of the medium is made strong and intense just because it is given another medium as content. The content of a movie is a novel or a play or an opera. The effect of the movie form is not related to its program content. The content of writing or print is speech, but the reader is almost entirely unaware either of print or of speech. Marshall McLuhan, *Understanding Media,* 1964

1965

Suddenly, articles on McLuhan began to appear in virtually every general-interest magazine, as well as intellectual reviews; a 1965 profile in New York magazine by Tom Wolfe—entitled "What if He Is Right?"—was particularly influential. Corporate leaders, government officials, educators, advertising and media executives sought him for lectures, Playboy magazine interviewed him, the popular television show Laugh-In made his name a catchphrase, intellectuals like Norman Mailer and Dwight MacDonald vehemently hailed or denounced him, John Lennon worshipfully came visiting, Abbie Hoffman regarded him as a prophet of the Woodstock Nation, and The New Yorker certified his status as cultural icon by citing him in cartoons. McLuhan's prediction that the new media would lead to a richer sensory balance and in-depth involvement in all aspects of life held immense appeal, particularly to youth. ⊙

McLuhanacy

Within popular culture, for those people who were members of the so-called television generation, a lot of what McLuhan had to say made a good deal of sense. Difficult to understand, not straightforward, not the kind of thing you learn by rote, but the kind of thing that really forced you to change your mind. I can't tell you how many people I've run across who can actually cite the moment they had some kind of breakthrough in understanding McLuhan. Their stories almost sound like religious experiences. Such responses to McLuhan terrified his critics because they thought this was McLuhanacy—that he was starting a kind of revolution or new religion.

McLuhan's insights were absorbed by members of the television generation. The kinds of metaphors that he came up with—such as the global village and the medium is the message—those metaphors never went away. Despite the excommunication of McLuhan by the academy, those metaphors continued to circulate. Other metaphors that seemed more coherent or more academically acceptable did not come along to replace those by McLuhan. That did not happen. There was a resonance between McLuhan's metaphors and the experiences that people were having. **Liss Jeffrey**

One of two cartoons The New Yorker ran on McLuhan in 1966; *opposite page, bottom left*: McLuhan with Rowan and Martin, the hosts of *Laugh-In*, one of his favourite shows.

Massage

"The medium is the message" is pregnant with all kinds of meanings. My father used this phrase as the title of a book that came out in the late sixties, only he gave it a little twist. He called the book *The Medium is the Massage*. There are four puns in that little phrase. First, "the medium is the message"—the familiar phrase. Split "message" into two words: mess-age. Every new medium makes a mess of the age. It messes up the current situation. The "massage": every new medium gives the culture a working over and a complete massage—both unexpected and unwanted. Then split "massage" into two words: mass-age— The medium is the mass age, meaning our present media and mass audiences. So there are four levels of meaning in that title, and he intended all four.

Eric McLuhan

Cult classic: first edition of *The Medium is the Massage*, 1967.

All situations are composed of an area of attention [figure] and a very much larger (subliminal) area of inattention [ground].... Figures rise out of, and recede back into, ground ... for example, at a lecture, the attention will shift from the speaker's words to his gestures, to the hum of the lighting or street sounds, or to the feel of the chair or a memory or association or smell, each new figure alternatively displaces the others into ground.... The ground of any technology is both the situation that gives rise to it as well as the whole environment (medium) of services and disservices that the technology brings with it. These are side effects and impose themselves willy-nilly as a new form of culture. The medium is the message. Marshall McLuhan and Eric McLuhan, *Laws of Media,* 1988

He used to say things like, "The medium is the message," and therefore, the content of the programming of any sort in any medium is fairly irrelevant. That sort of hyperbole goes a shade too far. I remember asking him, "Does that mean that the content of Homer's *Odyssey* is not very significant?" He said, "No, no, no. Not at all. But you can't even access the content unless you know that it is something that's coming to you through a bard or as an epic poem in print, or as a Hollywood film. How do you access the content if you don't know something about the medium first?" So he always went back to the medium to treat it as hidden ground. He loved investigating culture using the figure/ground relationships developed by Gestalt psychology. He always said that the out-of-awareness aspects of communication are where the action is. The content — where you're focused, where your attention is focused on the figure — is often almost meaningless. **Frank Zingrone**

He threw out paragraphs, probes, bits and pieces: McLuhan at the lectern, 1975.

He was such a delightful fellow. His mood was always elevated. I don't remember him being ordinary at any level at any time. He was always humorous and elevated. Sublime and ridiculous. Ridiculous because he could be ridiculous. Ridiculous in a totally charming way. He'd burp. He'd burp all the time. And he'd come up with the same old jokes all the time. And they were very endearing. Another thing about McLuhan that I found so important was the way he lived in what I call the absolute present. Absolutely there. Entirely in the moment. In a way that I can't even imitate. Artists are like that. Great artists are; they have this quality of just being there. **Derrick de Kerckhove**

The Shooting Line

The artist is the only person — his antennae pick up these messages before anybody. So he is always thought of as being way ahead of his time because he lives in the present. There are very many reasons why most people prefer to live in the age just behind them. It's safer. To live right on the shooting line, right on the frontier of change, is terrifying.

Marshall McLuhan, *The New Majority with Ed Fitzgerald,* CBC Television, 1970

McLuhan is like Picasso. He said, "I always paint fakes. I have painted two hundred paintings and five thousand are being sold in the States." There is an agreeable truth to what McLuhan said. But it has to do with freedom, a certain freedom of mind. The more McLuhan achieved a kind of playful freedom with his own thinking, the less consistent and substantial his books became. He began playing more and more with this idea of using chunks, facets of written material, instead of creating a theoretical, heavy-duty kind of volume. When we were working together on *From Cliché to Archetype,* he explained that you are basically the content of any medium you use. The user is the content. So when you get into *From Cliché to Archetype,* what you are doing is playing your experience and knowledge against the new combinations of thoughts that arise from these new bits and pieces of writings. You are the bond of the thoughts—you, the reader. The substance is provided by the reader. That method left a lot of academics uncomfortable, because it wasn't an academic approach. McLuhan was very fond of Dada, of absurdism, fond of the interplay of things that were not meant to be connected at first. He was fond of cutting loose the connections in systems. He often said you have to have a certain play between one and the other parts of whatever it is you're playing with. It has to give. If you don't have enough distance between the two objects of your attention, then there is no play, no place for the mind to make a discovery. It's so vacuous, there's nothing to play about. **Derrick de Kerckhove**

The entire literate and visual society of the Western world is being plunged into the intensely integral electrical cultural environment that is so profoundly oral and tribal. It is the Bergsons and the Picassos who have announced the literate plunge into the tribal experience. Nonliterate and nonvisual societies experience the same plunge as is encountered with literacy. Electric circuitry enables the East to experience the West as an environment, but the West is having the experience of involvement in the East by the same means at the same time. Marshall McLuhan, "Marshall McLuhan: The Man Who Infuriates the Critics," interview by Thomas P. McDonnell, *U.S. Catholic,* 1966

Among friends: *top:* McLuhan sketched by artist and writer Wyndham Lewis, 1944; *bottom:* relaxing with architect Buckminster Fuller, 1970.

He loved pronouncing upon things. And when people came to him and said, "Marshall, you are a guru," he said, existentially, "Yes, I am a guru and I will be a guru and I will respond like a guru." And that's pretty seductive stuff. He was damn good at it. What else does a guru do? He gives you poetry to deal with, which happens to be spiritually oriented rather than the give-and-take of daily communications. But yes, he loved to have people sit at his feet and often he himself was prone while they were doing so. As you know, he used to do a lot of his teaching from a reclined position, both at the Centre for Culture and Technology and on the couch in front of his fireplace, which was one of his favorite places in the world. And he loved you to sit there at his feet and he would pronounce, and he was sometimes a little crusty when you challenged him. But if you did it with good humor and kept at it, then he'd take up the game, and he was an awfully good game player. **Patrick Watson**

The percussed victims of the new technology have invariably muttered clichés about the impracticality of artists and their fanciful preferences. But in the past century, it has come to be generally acknowledged that, in the words of Wyndham Lewis, "The artist is always engaged in writing a detailed history of the future because he is the only person aware of the nature of the present." Knowledge of this simple fact is now needed for human survival. The ability of the artist to sidestep the bully blow of new technology of any age, and to parry such violence with full awareness, is age-old. Equally age-old is the inability of the percussed victims, who cannot sidestep the new violence, to recognize their need of the artist. To reward and to make celebrities of artists can, also, be a way of ignoring their prophetic work and preventing its timely use for survival. The artist is the man in any field, scientific or humanistic, who grasps the implications of his actions and of new knowledge in his own time. He is the man of integral awareness. Marshall McLuhan, *Understanding Media*, 1964

I have said that the medium is the message in the long run. It would be easy to explain and confirm this point historically. Print simply wiped out the main modes of oral education that had been devised in the Greco-Roman world and transmitted with the phonetic alphabet and the manuscript throughout the medieval period. And it ended that twenty-five-hundred-year pattern in a few decades. Today, the monarchy of print has ended and an oligarchy of new media has usurped most of the power of that five-hundred-year-old monarchy.

Marshall McLuhan, fourteenth National Conference on Higher Education, 1959

scenda x

eir unity of thought and action." On waltzing: "The Siamese Twins, suppleme

ry report" *Lancet* (4 Apr 1874) 493–94. On Hale: J.W. Hale to Charles Harris,

pt, 4 Nov and 14 Nov 1832, in the Papers of Dr. Charles Harris, Box 1 #5,

urmond Chatham Papers, P.C. 1139, and Chang-Eng, letter [in first person s

lar] to [Abel] Coffin, 22 Dec 1831, by the hand of Charles Harris, in Chang a

g Bunker, Siamese Twins Papers, P.C. 916, all at North Carolina State Archiv

Exter

Any extension, whether of skin, hand, or foot,
affects the whole psychic and social complex.

Marshall McLuhan, *Understanding Media*, 1964

sions of Man

MY
MAIN
THEME

s the extension of the nervous system in the electric age, and thus, the complete break with five thousand years of mechanical technology. This I state over and over again. I do not say whether it is a good or bad thing. To do so would be meaningless and arrogant.

Marshall McLuhan, letter to Robert Fulford, 1964

1967 In 1967 McLuhan accepted an invitation to teach for a year at New York's Fordham University. His time there was marked by perhaps the most painful experience of his life—an operation for the removal of a benign brain tumor at Columbia Presbyterian Medical Center in November 1967. For months, perhaps years, afterward, McLuhan suffered from extreme sensitivity to sounds and smells. Loud noises caused him agonies. In addition, he endured some memory loss, though mostly temporary. On the whole, however, he recovered quickly from the operation and resumed his teaching and writing when he returned to the University of Toronto in 1968. ⊙

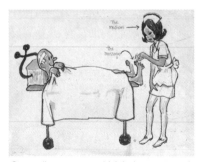

Get well soon: a card McLuhan received after his operation.

Auto-amputation

With the arrival of electric technology, man extended, or set outside himself, a live model of the central nervous system itself. To the degree that this is so, it is a development that suggests a desperate and suicidal auto-amputation, as if the central nervous system could no longer depend on the physical organs to be protective buffers against the slings and arrows of outrageous mechanism. It could well be that the successive mechanizations of the various physical organs since the invention of printing have made too violent and superstimulated a social experience for the central nervous system to endure. Marshall McLuhan, *Understanding Media*, 1964

I don't think there is a new understanding of his message; I think people are just looking at it again and reexamining it. I don't think there is *a* message; I think there are a lot of little different messages. There is no one grand theory of communication to be found in McLuhan. McLuhan didn't think that way. He thought like a poet; he thought in terms of individual ideas and images. Global village is the classic example. **Robert Fulford**

Servomechanisms

To behold, use, or perceive any extension of ourselves in technological form is necessarily to embrace it. To listen to radio or to read the printed page is to accept these extensions of ourselves into our personal system and to undergo the closure or displacement of perception that follows automatically. It is this continuous embrace of our own technology in daily use that puts us in the Narcissus role of subliminal awareness and numbness in relation to these images of ourselves. By continuously embracing technologies, we relate ourselves to them as servomechanisms. That is why we must, to use them at all, serve these objects, these extensions of ourselves, as gods or minor religions. An Indian is the servomechanism of his canoe, as the cowboy of his horse or the executive of his clock. Marshall McLuhan, *Understanding Media*, 1964

McLuhan is a difficult read, in a sense, because he uses satire; he called his method Manipian satire. This method is illustrated in some of his comments, some of his more extreme comments. For example, when he says we become the servomechanisms of our technologies, he's not celebrating that. What he's doing is pointing out that this is in fact how things work—that those of us who are addicted to constantly communicating must have the telephone growing out of our ears (or, in my case, a pen growing out of my hand)—and if we think about it we begin to see that there is some sense to that. Also, what tends to happen with McLuhan is that it's forgotten that one of his chief insights was, "It's not my private opinions that are important, what's important is to pay attention to what's going on." He repeated insistently that we should stop saying, "Is this a good thing or a bad thing?" and start saying, "What's going on?" Then we could come up with something relevant. **Liss Jeffrey**

When the motorcar was new, it exercised the typical mechanical pressure of explosion and separation of functions. It broke up family life, or so it seemed, in the 1920s. It separated work and domicile as never before. It exploded each city into a dozen suburbs and then extended many of the forms of urban life along the highways until the open road seemed to become nonstop cities. It created the asphalt jungles and caused 40,000 square miles of green and pleasant land to be cemented over. Marshall McLuhan, *Understanding Media*, 1964

The American Way

It [on ground] is a term from Gestalt psychology. Look at the ground around the figure of the automobile or the ground around any technology, which necessarily has a large ground of services and disservices associated with it. Now, the ordinary attention is fixed on the figure rather than the ground, on the wheel rather than the huge system of road services necessary to maintain the existence of a wheel or wheeled vehicles. With a motorcar, most people are interested in changing designs or patterns of the car. They pay only incidental attentions to the huge service environment of roads, oil companies, filling stations, and other allied services of manufacturing that are the ground of the car.

The motorcar, when it was first introduced in the early part of the century, was thought to be a sure way of getting rid of cities by taking us back to the country. Watching the figure of the car, they saw the immediate possibility of simply transporting city dwellers back into the country where they came from. An early phrase about the motorcar was, "Let's take a spin in the country." It never occurred to them that this figure of the car might generate a huge ground of new services far bigger that the figure was ever thought to be. In other words, the car created a totally new environment or ground of services and disservices that we have come to associate with the American way of life.

By not looking at the ground around the automobile you miss the message of the car. For it is the ground of any technology that is the medium that changes everybody, and it is the medium that is the message of the technology, not the figure.

Marshall McLuhan, "Marshall McLuhan," interview by Willem L. Oltmans, 1972

The abrasive interplay and collision of perceptions in the TV medium fostered new kinds of dialogue and awareness on the part of the TV users. The TV user is the content of TV. Everybody who exists within any man-made service environment experiences all the effects that he would undergo in any environment as such. Environments work us over and remake us. It is man who is the content of the message of the media, which are extensions of himself. Electronic man must know the effects of the world he has made, above all things.

Marshall McLuhan and Barrington Nevitt, *Take Today: The Executive as Dropout*, 1972

Marshall did not believe in research; he did not believe in testing. If someone appeared to contradict his ideas, he would simply change the subject rather than testing it and pushing it and altering it. Just as you can't contradict a poem and you can't contradict a painting, you couldn't really contradict one of his ideas. Nor could you test it. His whole life, he was being educated and reeducated. **Robert Fulford**

McLuhan was perpetually looking up words in the Oxford English Dictionary, savoring their etymology. When he read James Joyce's Finnegans Wake, *he immediately recognized a soul mate. Joyce, too, loved puns and believed that the archaic meanings of words were never wholly lost, contributing to the powerful spell of language. Sometimes, McLuhan pushed this sense of word magic — it was akin to the primitive belief that a name expresses the essence of a thing — to eccentric lengths. He once remarked that the name of a man is a numbing blow from which he never recovers. He believed, for example, that Richard Nixon was deeply affected by the negative connotations of the first syllable of his last name.* ⊙

One of McLuhan's most famous theories is that polarity between hot and cold, which he used to analyze television. It was also used by the American media to explain why John Kennedy did so well in the first debate that he had with Richard Nixon. People say that those who happened to listen to that debate on the radio felt that Nixon had won. Those who watched on television thought that Kennedy had resoundingly defeated Nixon. What McLuhan began to see is that style is substance in many ways in modern times. People feel uneasy about this because they feel that surely it means the rise of another Hitler and Stalin. I say no to such a conclusion. I believe that the television camera coming so close to a person's face finally tells you the truth. The camera does not lie over time. You can manipulate a political advertisement. You can do all kinds of cutting. But a camera just trained on a person in a long debate of the Nixon versus Kennedy kind — or following candidates through a period, through the primaries, through all the things that can come at you, and you're exhausted and you're going from state to state and never have enough sleep — is the best indicator yet that we have of the character of a person. **Camille Paglia**

TV is a cool medium. It rejects hot figures and hot issues and people from the hot press media. Fred Allen was a casualty of TV. Was Marilyn Monroe? Had TV occurred on a large scale during Hitler's reign he would have vanished quickly. Had TV come first there would have been no Hitler at all. When Khrushchev appeared on American TV, he was more acceptable than Nixon as a clown and a lovable sort of old boy. His appearance is rendered by TV as a comic cartoon. Radio, however, is a hot medium and takes cartoon characters seriously. Mr. K. on radio would be a different proposition.

Marshall McLuhan, *Understanding Media*, 1964

We may be approaching the time when political and executive figures may have to be recruited on the same basis as was formerly used for movie stars. Alternatively, it might be possible to transfer the Paul Newmans or the John Waynes from the entertainment sphere to the political sphere directly in order to satisfy the need of people to be reassured by images that remind them of all the people they might have been in some ideal existence.

Marshall McLuhan, unpublished essay, 1974

In terms of the theme of media hot and cold, backward countries are cool and we are hot. The city slicker is hot and the rustic is cool. But in terms of the reversal of procedures and values in the electric age, the past mechanical time was hot and we of the TV age are cool. The waltz was a hot, fast, mechanical dance suited to the industrial time in its moods of pomp and circumstance. In contrast, the Twist is a cool, involved, and chatty form of improvised gesture. The jazz of the period of the hot new media of movie and radio was hot jazz. Yet jazz of itself tends to be a casual dialogue form of dance quite lacking in the repetitive and mechanical forms of the waltz. Cool jazz came in quite naturally after the first impact of radio and movie had been absorbed.

Marshall McLuhan, *Understanding Media*, 1964

The effects of television have reshaped everything and we've become more and more aware that the broadcast media has totally taken over. Since Reagan, since Clinton, there's no pretense anymore that anything other than television is the be-all and end-all of politics. Not just because politicians get on television, but because television shapes our habits in how we look at them. Way back in the seventies, McLuhan said, "A politician's image is going to be much more important than the politician himself." This was way before Reagan, way before Clinton. Way before today's politicians became a living demonstration of McLuhan's words. **Philip Marchand**

Hot And Cool

There is a basic principle that distinguishes a hot medium like radio from a cool one like the telephone, or a hot medium like the movie from a cool one like TV. A hot medium is one that extends one single sense in high definition. High definition is the state of being well filled with data. A photograph is, visually, high definition. A cartoon is low definition, simply because very little visual information is provided. Telephone is a cool medium, or one of low definition, because the ear is given a meager amount of information. And speech is a cool medium of low definition, because so little is given and so much has to be filled in by the listener. On the other hand, hot media do not leave so much to be filled in or completed by the audience. Hot media are, therefore, low in participation, and cool media are high in participation or completion by the audience. Naturally, therefore, a hot medium like radio has very different effects on the user from a cool medium like the telephone. Marshall McLuhan, *Understanding Media*, 1964

I would say McLuhan was a great thinker, then add: there are many rooms in the house of the intellect. And different kinds of thinkers occupy different kinds of rooms. If there's a room for those thinkers who see something quite differently from everyone else, and form a question that people in the other rooms hadn't thought about, in that sense we could say McLuhan was a great thinker. I don't think we would call him a great scholar because I don't think he really had the patience to work through some of the implications of what he was saying, even in a book like *The Gutenberg Galaxy*. It also has to be added that there was more than a touch of poet in him, as everyone who knew him will tell you. Some of his ideas have almost a poetic import to them, as distinct from a researchable, definable context. I have no hesitation using the term great thinker to describe McLuhan, provided people understand that there are different kinds of great thinkers. **Neil Postman**

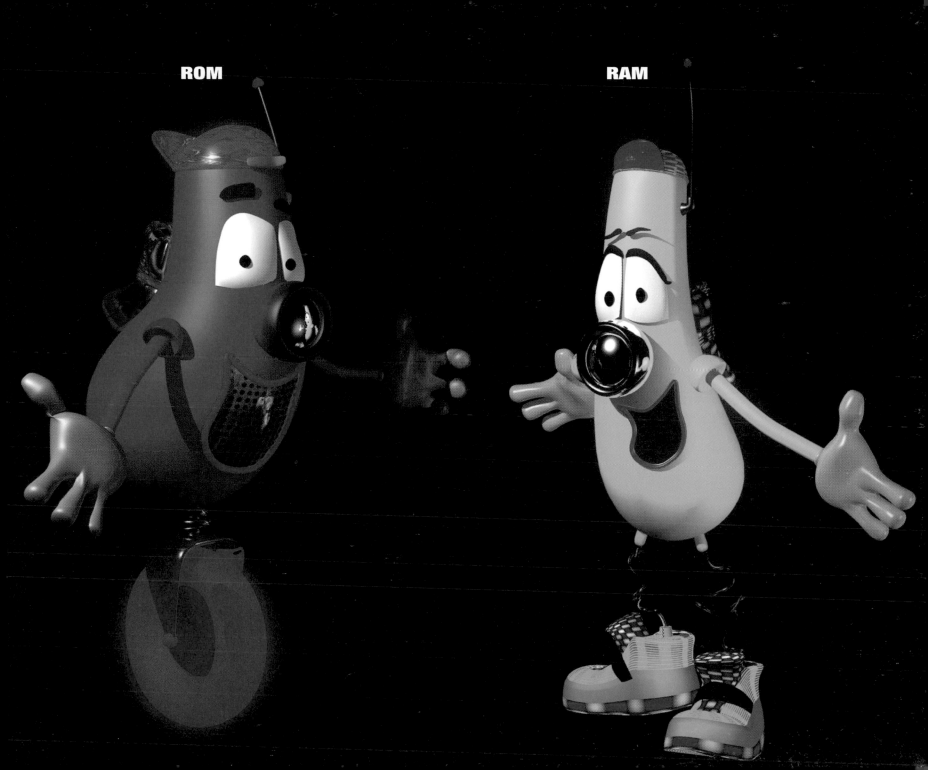

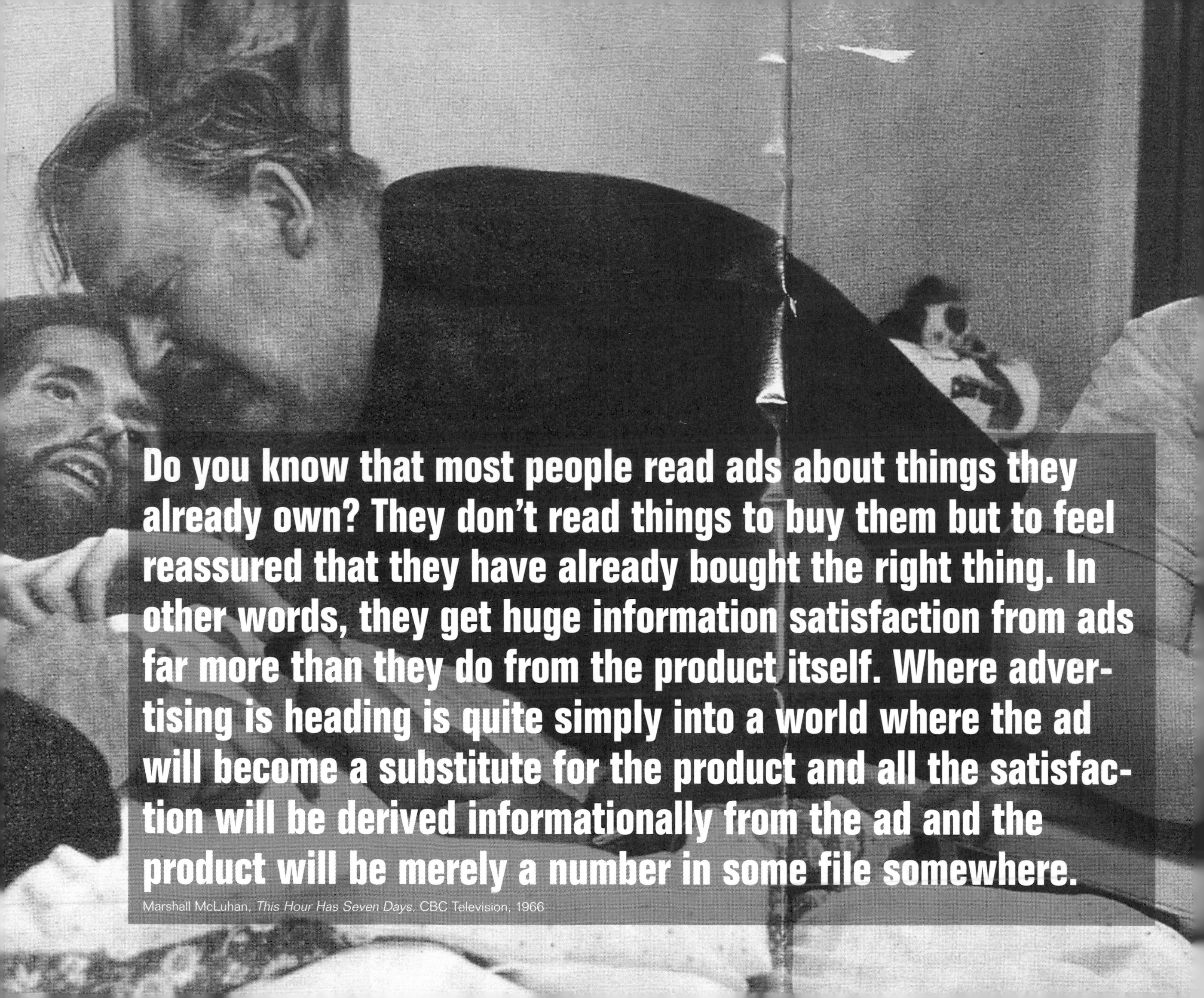

Do you know that most people read ads about things they already own? They don't read things to buy them but to feel reassured that they have already bought the right thing. In other words, they get huge information satisfaction from ads far more than they do from the product itself. Where advertising is heading is quite simply into a world where the ad will become a substitute for the product and all the satisfaction will be derived informationally from the ad and the product will be merely a number in some file somewhere.

Marshall McLuhan, *This Hour Has Seven Days*, CBC Television, 1966

Ads Are News

The ads are by far the best part of any magazine or news-paper. More pain and thought, more wit and art, go into the making of an ad than into any prose feature of press or magazine. Ads are news. What is wrong with them is that they are always good news. In order to balance off the effect and to sell good news, it is necessary to have a lot of bad news. Moreover, the newspaper is a hot medium. It has to have bad news for the sake of inten-sity and reader participation. Real news is bad news, as already noted, and as any newspaper from the beginning of print can testify. Floods, fires, and other communal disasters by land and sea and air outrank any kind of private horror or villainy as news. Ads, in contrast, have to shrill their happy message loud and clear in order to match the penetrating power of bad news.

Marshall McLuhan, *Understanding Media,* 1964

Many people have expressed uneasiness about the advertising enterprise in our time. To put the matter abruptly, the advertising industry is a crude attempt to extend the principles of automation to every aspect of society. Ideally, advertising aims at the goal of a pro-grammed harmony among all human impulses and aspi-rations and endeavors. Using handicraft methods, it stretches out towards the ultimate electronic goal of a collective consciousness. When all production and all consumption are brought into a preestablished harmony with all desire and all effort, then advertising will have liquidated itself by its own success.

Marshall McLuhan, *Understanding Media,* 1964

I think his ongoing legacy will be as somebody who had an early and prescient understanding of the nature of the mass media, the electronic media, and what the likely effect of those media would be on society and its habits of thought and styles of feeling. It was McLuhan's phrase "we make our tools and then our tools shape us." And so first we make the tool of print and movable type and we get used to that way of seeing and arranging our ideas and our thoughts. Then this gives way, four hundred years later, to the electronic means of communication and media is used almost as a way of transporting information and ideas and feelings. McLuhan talked about the media as if it were canals or roads or highways; he talked about it in a very practical, literal way. Once we get used to using these media, our tools shape us and that then leads to different habits of thought. I think that's happening. An understanding of McLuhan helps me to understand why our politics are what they are, why our entertainments are what they are, why our literary forms are not the way they were twenty or thirty years ago. People now tend to write in much shorter lengths and, once you have photography and once you have television, you don't need Dickens to explain what the lower depths of London look like, so it shifts our means of expression as well as our means of perception. To read McLuhan is to understand in a way why Bill Clinton was elected president of the United States, why *Pulp Fiction* was the most interesting movie of its season. **Lewis Lapham**

The press can be seen in relation to figure and ground, and in psychology, as well as in journalism, the ground is usually subliminal relative to the figure. Under conditions of electric simultaneity, the ground of any figure tends to become more and more noticeable. Perhaps it all began with cubism and the discovery that by eliminating the merely visual or rational relations between services, by presenting the inside and the underside at the same time as the outside, the public became totally involved and aware in a multisensuous way.

Marshall McLuhan, "At the moment of Sputnik," *Journal of Communications*, 1974

Symbolist Poem

Let us look at the image of the newspaper as it still is today after a century of the telegraph. That image is organized not according to a story line but according to a dateline. Like a symbolist poem, the ordinary newspaper page is an assembly of unconnected items in abstract mosaic form. Looked at in this way, it is plain that the newspaper had been a corporate poem for many years. It represents an inclusive image of community and a wide diversity of human interests. Minus the story line of the connected narrative, the newspaper has long had an oral and corporate quality that relates it to many of the traditional art forms of mankind. On every page of the newspaper, in the discontinuous mosaic of unrelated human items, there is a resonance that bespeaks universality, even in triviality.

Marshall McLuhan, "At the moment of Sputnik," *Journal of Communications,* 1974

Obsolete

1967 *McLuhan perhaps abetted the decline of his reputation by turning out books deliberately aimed at cashing in on his boom. From 1967 to 1972, nine books appeared with his name on them. Often written with collaborators, they struck readers, for the most part, as obsessive and willfully obscure. In truth, McLuhan—particularly at this stage of his career—hated writing and had no idea how to shape a book. His preferred mode of expressing himself remained the spoken word.*

Meanwhile, McLuhan began to take a darker view of the media. He had never been a strong fan of television. His chief—almost his sole—recreation had been reading and talking, and when he did watch television he usually limited himself to lighter fare like Hogan's Heroes. *Always a staunch Catholic, he was generally dismayed by the casual attitude toward sex and drugs taken by television's children. Eventually, he developed the notion that any beneficial effects of a television-induced sensory shift had been nullified by the introduction of what he called disincarnate man. The constant broadcast and reception of ghostly images via radio and television, according to this notion, had weakened the sense, particularly among youth, of possessing physical bodies and private identities. Private morality, he believed, was passé—only tribal affiliations counted in the global village.* ☉

You know, there's an old saying in the business world, If it works, it's obsolete. And it's only when a thing has become obsolete that everybody is sufficiently familiar with it to make it work. Our motorcars were obsolete long ago, but that means they are really going concerns. There is more writing today than there was before Gutenberg, more handwriting. Obsolescence does not mean the conclusion but rather the beginning of a process as far as everyday life is concerned. This is not ordinarily understood. Most people think obsolescence means the end. It means the beginning. People always live with obsolescent attitudes and in obsolescent frames of mind and obsolescent technologies and homes.

Marshall McLuhan, *The New Majority with Ed Fitzgerald*, CBC Television, 1970

I almost think that the thing McLuhan would want to have as a lasting legacy is his insistence that people try to understand their environment more clearly, and that they not substitute moral judgment for insight into what is actually happening.

I've noticed since writing *The Medium and the Messenger* that when people talk about media or society there's always a moral tone to it. As if by making a moral statement they establish the fact that they are moral people, and that they are serious people. McLuhan always thought such behavior was an evasion of the worst sort. As he used to say, "Moral indignation is a technique used to endow the idiot with dignity." I think he certainly has left us an example of a kind of mind that can at least make a serious attempt to look at things freshly.

Philip Marchand

1977

Slowly, McLuhan's notoriety began to fade, interrupted only by episodes such as his appearance in Woody Allen's 1977 film Annie Hall and the odd profile in People magazine. As the seventies wore on, it became increasingly apparent that the apocalypse was no longer at hand. Feminism and the gay-rights movement marched on, but society absorbed such changes without overthrowing its basic institutions. Students continued to go to classrooms, and men and women still went to work in offices. Many of McLuhan's observations were vindicated—for example, the truth of his remark, made in the early seventies, that the image of a politician would be much more powerful than the politician himself—but the sixties revolutions had passed and so had the urgent desire for explanation of social change. The media had now "done" McLuhan thoroughly, and there seemed no need to return to the subject. ⊙

"I happen to have Mr. McLuhan right here," said Woody Allen in his 1977 film, *Annie Hall*.

"Beware clarity," he used to say. "A man speaking to you in clear language is clearly using obsolete ideas." Well, that threw people off. People said, "What do you mean? We love clarity." The other thing was that the world was in love with specialism. They were telling their kids to be specialists. You must be a specialist if you want to survive. McLuhan said the age of specialism was over. That made people very angry. They didn't understand that he was talking about the effects of electronic process ending the possibility that specialist knowledge from any one discipline could solve any of our problems. He would just point to what's really happening. He'd say, "This is a think tank. You can't solve any problems without having fourteen people from fourteen different disciplines all talking to each other trying to come up with a big-patterned solution to the problem. You don't call in one guy who is one specialist from one discipline and have him solve a problem. That's not the way it works." People didn't want to hear that. **Frank Zingrone**

As automation takes hold, it becomes obvious that information is the crucial commodity and that solid products are merely incidental to information movement. The early stages by which information itself became the basic economic commodity of the electric age were obscured by the ways in which advertising and entertainment put people off the track. Advertisers pay for space and time in paper and magazine, on radio and TV; that is, they buy a piece of the reader, listener, or viewer as definitely as if they hired our homes for a public meeting. They would gladly pay the reader, listener, or viewer directly for his time and attention if they knew how to do so. The only way so far devised is to put on a free show. Movies in America have not developed advertising intervals simply because the movie itself is the greatest of all forms of advertisement for consumer goods. Marshall McLuhan, *Understanding Media*, 1964

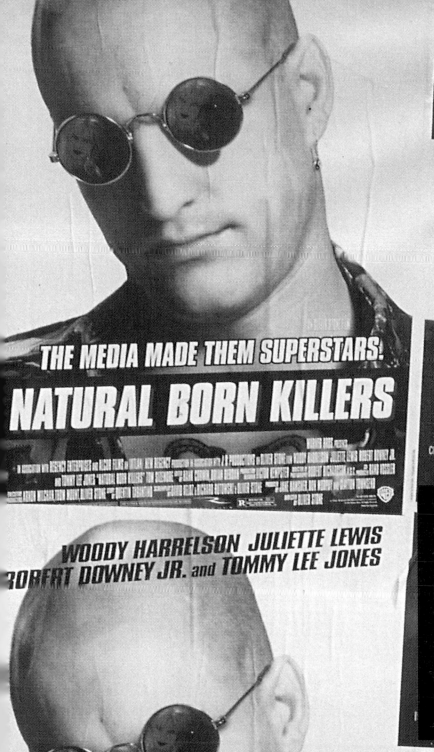
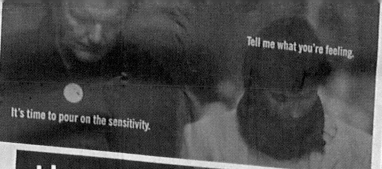

We are swiftly moving at present from an era when business was our culture into an era when culture will be our business. Between these poles stand the huge and ambiguous entertainment industries. As the new media unfold their powers, the entertainment industries swallow more and more of the old business culture. The movie industry is thus an inseparable portion of the advertising industry in providing the necessary drama of consumption, in which the ads merely provide the news. Marshall McLuhan, unpublished essay, 1957

Every Kid Knows

Jobs are finished; role-playing has taken over; the job is a passé entity. The job belonged to the specialist. The kids know that they no longer live in a specialist world; you cannot have a goal today. You cannot say, "I'm going to start here and I'm going to work for the next three years and I'm going to go all that distance." Every kid knows that within three years, everything will have changed — including himself and the goal.

Marshall McLuhan with A. F. Knowles, *York University Instructional Services Video*, 1971

Marshall McLuhan said something like, Men are suddenly nomadic gatherers of knowledge, nomadic as never before. What is a person who uses the Internet, surfing for knowledge and information? Man, he understood the Internet. He *was* the Internet in the sixties. The world's just finally caught up to him. He was an internet in the sense he was in touch with the entire globe. For some reason, this man had his fingers in everything. He was wired long before the editors of *Wired* magazine were born. This man was truly wired. **Robert Logan**

Interior spread from *The Medium is the Massage,* 1967.

I went to college in 1967 and graduated in 1971. That period was around when McLuhan's influence was at its peak; it was certainly incredibly influential on my thinking about life. So I've carried the seeds of McLuhan and McLuhanism, throughout my entire adult life. *Wired* is about media today—about how we live in the media environment, how the media environment affects our lives. If there is a prophet of new media—radio, television, networking, interactivity—it has to be that man. There is no other single individual who had such a clear vision of where we were going. And so to me it was totally natural that as we were looking for examples of what *Wired* should look like, I went back to my bookshelf and pulled out a copy of *The Medium is the Massage,* and went through it page by page again. It's so dynamic it could have been published yesterday. It's still as fresh as it ever was, and it's certainly something that stimulated us to think about how to use the print medium today to talk about changes that are occurring in other media. So for all those reasons it seemed completely normal for us to say that Marshall McLuhan was our patron saint, as he should be for the entire media revolution that's going on now. **Louis Rossetto**

The wired planet has no boundaries and no monopolies of knowledge. The affairs of the world are now dependent upon the highest information of which man is capable.... The boundaries between the world of affairs and the community of learning have ceased to exist. The workaday world now demands encyclopedic wisdom. Ecology is the simultaneous awareness of the interplay of the total field of processes. This simultaneity pushes the most banal situations into high relevance. Under these conditions, the old forms of specialized job has lost meaning. It was meaningful only at very low speeds, but it has now been assumed into patterns of electric speeds. This change of pace from production line to on-line computer programming has been ignored, just as the shift from hardware to software accelerates, making the old categories meaningless. Marshall McLuhan and Barrington Nevitt, *Take Today: The Executive as Dropout,* 1972

1980 *McLuhan continued teaching at the University of Toronto and holding his seminars every year, until he suffered a debilitating stroke in September 1979. The man who lived for talking and communicating could now utter only a few phrases. In 1980, the university, hard-pressed for funds, closed down the Centre for Culture and Technology. McLuhan showed up one evening and wept because his old office was in shambles. He could do nothing, however, to reclaim his old life, and his ordeal continued until, some time early in the morning of December 31, 1980, he died in bed at his Toronto home.* ☉

There was a period when he was the most talked-about intellectual on the planet. And then, long before he died, all that went away. Many people turned against him because they found his ideas didn't hold up or didn't fit with their thinking. They found that he was too opportunistic; they found that he would fling off an idea at random without thinking about it. They found that he was too easy to buy, he was too available on the speech-giving circuit, and somehow a bad aura collected around him for those and probably fifty other reasons.
Philip Marchand

Today, as the new vortices of power are shaped by the instant electric interdependence of all men on this planet, the visual factor in social organization and in personal experience recedes and money begins to be less and less a means of storing or exchanging work and skill. Automation, which is electronic, does not represent physical work so much as programmed knowledge. As work is replaced by the sheer movement of information, money as a store of work merges with the informational forms of credit and credit card. From coin to paper currency, and from currency to credit card, there is a steady progression towards commercial exchange as the movement of information itself.

Marshall McLuhan, *Understanding Media*, 1964

Marshall was a publicity hound; he was the professor as self-promoter. At the beginning of his career, he imagined that he would make a lot of money selling his ideas to business and industry, perhaps governments. He imagined that he was such an idea man that his ideas would flow out and people would buy them. And in order to do that he had to be famous; he *wanted* to be famous. Fame was not thrust upon him; he sought it, and sought it with great care.
Robert Fulford

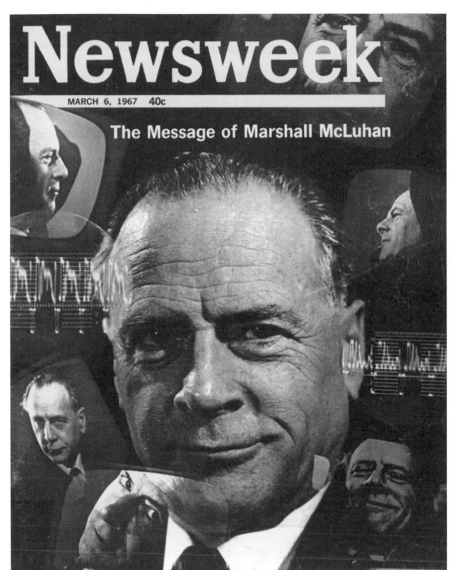

Newsweek

MARCH 6, 1967 40c

The Message of Marshall McLuhan

The most talked about intellectual on the planet: *left to right*: McLuhan makes the cover of *Newsweek* in March 1967; McLuhan receives the Companion of the Order of Canada in Ottawa, 1975; McLuhan with luminaries W. H. Auden (second from left) and Buckminster Fuller (second from right).

McLuhan with Buckminster Fuller in the Bahamas, 1970.

McLuhan was very much a product of his time in the way that he and others like him—people like Northrop Frye and Harold Innis—were able to look at things from a global perspective. I don't see anyone doing that now. Everything has become parochial. Canada is a much more regionalized country than it was in McLuhan's time, the United States is domestically much more provincial, while the whole world is embracing, to some extent, separatism. Yet, in an interesting sort of way, McLuhan's vision of technology is uniting us. I suppose you could say that he allowed for the imploding of national perspectives—at least the kinds he was familiar with. **John Fraser**

Cottage

The computer could become the basis of a cottage economy again. Just as the kids have gone back to the Middle Ages in their costumes and social outlook, so our economy could return to a cottage economy of a much earlier time. You could run the world's biggest factory in a kitchen by a computer. With telephones, telexes, and computers—all of which operate at instant speeds—management and all forms of hardware can be centralized. The computer, literally, could run the world from a cottage. Marshall McLuhan, *The New Majority with Ed Fitzgerald*, CBC Television, 1970

Filing Cabinet

In our own world, we are hurrying back and forth across town at morning and night to situations we could easily encompass by closed circuit. Why do the wheels keep hurrying us downtown? Some people are puzzled by this and have come up with the answer: it's the filing cabinet downtown in the offices that makes it still necessary to rush back and forth from suburb to office. That it is this obsession with the contents of the file — documents, contracts, data. All of these materials actually could be just as available on closed circuit at home.

Marshall McLuhan, *Take Thirty*, CBC Television, 1965

Banana-Skin Pirouette

Electric technology is directly related to our central nervous systems, so it is ridiculous to talk of what the public wants played over its nerves. This question would be like asking people what sort of sights and sounds they would prefer around them in an urban metropolis! Once we have surrendered our senses and nervous systems to the private manipulation of those who would try to benefit from taking a lease on our eyes and ears and nerves, we don't really have any rights left. Leasing our eyes and ears and nerves to commercial interests is like handing over the common speech to a private corporation, or like giving the earth's atmosphere to a company as a monopoly. Something like this has already happened with outer space for the same reasons that we have leased our central nervous systems to various corporations. As long as we adopt the Narcissus attitude of regarding the extensions of our own bodies as really out there and really independent of us, we will meet all technological challenges with the same sort of banana-skin pirouette and collapse.

Marshall McLuhan, *Understanding Media*, 1964

1993 Throughout the eighties, McLuhan's name appeared in print almost solely in connection with his phrase *global village, as if this were his only legacy. In the early nineties, however, his reputation began to rise again. The popular high-tech magazine* Wired, *founded in 1993—the most influential new periodical of the decade—signaled this revival by putting his name on its masthead as "patron saint." In the fall of 1994, The MIT Press reissued McLuhan's* Understanding Media, *with a new preface by the noted American editor and commentator Lewis Lapham.* ☉

DERRICK MAY ·TRANSMAT RECORDS.

WESTBAM ·LOV

DJ SONIC ·OMNISONUS..

DOC MARTIN ·LOS

SCOTT HARDKISS ·HARDKISS MUSIC...SAN FRANCIS

MARK FARINA ·MUSHROOM JAZ

JOHN HOWARD ·SAN

CORY ·VAN

ROBERT SHEA ·HARTHOU

LIVE ACT **BT** ·PERFE

LIVE ACT

LIVE ACT **DUBTRIBE** ·DU

DER DRITTE RAUM ·HARTHOUSE

PSYCHIC WARRIORS OF GAÏA ·KK R

LIVE ACT

On the left margin (partial text, cut off):

ROIT

IT...BERLIN

S

LES

N FRANCISCO

CISCO

JDGE...SAN FRANCISCO

CORDS...LOS ANGELES

ECORDS...UK

SOUND SYSTEM...SAN FRANCISCO

DS...FRANKFURT

S...HOLLAND

We, today, in the electric age are about as primitive as any Eskimo ever was when he saw his first railway. Our ability to cope with this new electronic technology is not any greater than that. Marshall McLuhan, *The Best of Ideas*, CBC Radio, 1967

McLuhan was very definitely a renegade, a guy doing something that almost nobody else seems inclined to do. Camille Paglia says, "I'm his number-one fan. I'm a big student of McLuhan's." But what she does isn't quite what McLuhan did. Not quite. She doesn't have the training that he had in the arts and the tradition, or the years, to practice it.

One reason, I think, that McLuhan is being rediscovered is that although all the media he talked about—television and film and radio and satellites—are still here, the world has changed. The things that McLuhan talked about are still causing trouble and raising questions. He showed twenty or thirty years ago how to study these issues, and when you apply his techniques to these things today, you get contemporary answers.

There's another reason for McLuhan's rediscovery: since 1980, an amazing number of new media have appeared, like the personal desktop computer, which we all take for granted. PCs have been around only about half a generation, which seems incredible because we're so accustomed to them. Here we are surrounded by a whole pile of new media: PCs and faxes, videoconferencing, virtual reality, CDs, and CD-ROMs. The LP record is gone. Fifteen years ago, it was in its heyday. Nothing was going to happen to it. All kinds of things have happened in the meantime, and nobody else is studying them. Well, that leaves the field rather free for old McLuhan to resurface and say, "Look here. Here's how you should do it. Here's where you look. Here's the kind of thing that you've got to keep your eye on and here are the distractions. Here are the things to ignore. Now go for it." **Eric McLuhan**

In the end, it's not about technology, it's about the connection of people to people. Technology itself enables this connection. It's a channel for individual and social expression. McLuhan recognized that this is the importance of technology. He recognized that technology is the campfire of the global village.

Louis Rossetto

NO MORE HISTORY

When you hear the word progress, you know you are dealing with a nineteenth-century mind. Progress literally stopped with electricity because you now have everything at once. You don't move on from one thing at a time to the next thing. There is no more history; it's all here. There isn't any part of the past that isn't with us, thanks to electricity. But it's not thanks to print, it's not thanks to photography, it's thanks to electricity. Speed, huge speed-up, means there's no more past. Now, there is no more history. Marshall McLuhan, *Ideas,* CBC Radio, 1969

Predicting The Present

He never predicted the future, never tried to. That was one of the things that irritated people. He said, "No. There are a lot of people busy predicting the future. I'll leave them to it, the futurologists and certain sociologists. That's their job, to look at the future. Historians take care of the past. I'll tackle the really tough one: the present. Let me see if I can predict the present." Which is damn near impossible. So he spent his time trying to "predict" the present, not the future. He often remarked that "the future is easy; it is anybody's game. But looking at the present and predicting that—that's difficult. That's what I want to do." Everything he said wasn't a prediction of what would happen but of what was just happening at the time.

But if you take those same techniques and turn them on the world and use them just as a means of finding out what is going on around you, then you've got McLuhan's whole technique. He didn't romanticize about the future or sentimentalize the past. He just worked on the present and found that a full-time occupation. **Eric McLuhan**

A friend has said the future of the future is the present. If you really are curious about the future, just study the present. Because what we ordinarily see in any present is really what appears in the rearview mirror. What we ordinarily think of as present is really the past. Modern suburbia lives in *Bonanza* land. It looks back nostalgically and sentimentally to the frontier as a safe and, at the same time, admirable and desirable world. This habit of seeing back one stage when thinking that one is looking at the present is an age-old human habit. And it may be that we are the first to discover a means of overcoming the limitations of this habit.

Marshall McLuhan, *The Best of Ideas,* CBC Radio, 1967

People never want to look at the present; people live in the rearview mirror because it's safer, they've been there before, they feel comfort. Anybody who looks at the present is a threat, a nuisance in the extremist degree. The present is an area that people have always avoided throughout human history — the utopias of mankind are all rearview-mirror images of the preceding age.

Marshall McLuhan, *The Seven O'Clock Show*, CBC Television, 1967

McLuhan promoting his work at a Montreal advertising luncheon, 1966.

I can't think of a book that I've written, that I could have written, if not for McLuhan. Which is not to say that he approved of any of my books he might have read, or would approve of others that he never did read. But as far as I'm concerned, I have always felt that the question he asked that is his main contribution is embedded in every idea that formed a book for me — whether I was writing about media in *Amusing Ourselves to Death,* or writing about language in *Crazy Talk, Stupid Talk,* or writing about education in *Teaching as a Subversive Activity.* And the question is something like: Does the form of any medium of communication affect our social relations, our political ideas, or psychic habits, and, of course, as he always emphasized, our sensorium? Once you have a question like that you can look at almost any social institution and put that question at the center of it. And I think I've done that in every book I've written. The first book I wrote was for the National Council of Teachers of English and it was about television — it was called *Television and the Teaching of English.* And I know I couldn't have written that book if I hadn't known about McLuhan. My career as a writer and teacher and social critic has been dependent on McLuhan, what I call McLuhan's question. **Neil Postman**

Big Book

McLuhan made a horrible mistake — he didn't write the "big book." He didn't write the book that takes four or five years in which you test your ideas and you find out which ones are meaningless and which are valid. You sort the good ones from the bad ones and try and build a synthesis out of a career of thinking. He didn't write that book, so there's nowhere that his admirers can tell people to go and say, Read that — that's what McLuhan's got to say to you. And so a century from now, it will be very hard for people to understand why we were excited about McLuhan. And I get the sense, even now, that a lot of feeling about McLuhan — gratitude to him, all knowledge of him — is oral. **Robert Fulford**

war and peace in the global village MARSHALL McLUHAN QUENTIN FIORE

VANISHING POINT

McLUHAN and PARK

The Medium is the Massage McLuhan Fiore NON-FICTION

MARSHALL McLUHAN | THE GUTENBERG GALAXY 451-Y3913-

SHALL McLUHAN

DERSTANDING MEDIA

There are different reasons for McLuhan's revival. For the first time since television achieved domination of the culture in the fifties and sixties, there is a new wave of technological innovation that seems on the verge of radically remaking our world—a wave signified by the Internet and virtual reality. Personal computers, first used largely as glorified typewriters, now seem capable of linking individuals into an electronic, instantaneous, global communication network.

These developments have sharpened our belief that an old-fashioned, content-based approach is inadequate to understanding technology. A comprehensive, effects-oriented approach—an attempt to grasp the whole pattern of change, including the innumerable and often ignored side effects of technological development—seems much more fitting. McLuhan is the master of this approach. ⊙

Religious Age

Many people simply resort instantly to the occult, to ESP, and every form of hidden awareness in answer to this new surround of electric consciousness. And so we live, in the vulgar sense, in an extremely religious age, and I think we are moving into an age that, in the popular notion at least, is probably the most religious that has ever existed. We are already there.

Marshall McLuhan, "Electric Consciousness and the Church," interview by Herbert Hoskins, *The Listener,* 1970

One of the effects of living with electric information is that we live habitually in a state of information overload. There's always more than you can cope with.

Marshall McLuhan, *The Best of Ideas,* CBC Radio, 1967

The eighties will see a great swing from the military towards the temple bureaucracy, from the outer conquest of space to the inner conquest of spirit. Holy wars will occur—an extreme example of hardware shifting to software and spiritual values.

Marshall McLuhan, "Living at the Speed of Light," *Maclean's* magazine, 1980

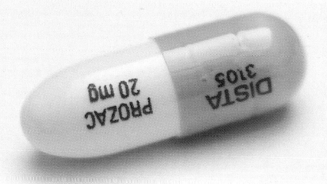

The electronic environment of information is an incubus. It settles upon the human sensorium like a fungus. It transforms every mode of our experience totally. This terrifies people. They prefer to forget.

Marshall McLuhan, *The Seven O'Clock Show*, CBC Television, 1967

McLuhan's revival has to do with the fact that the more profound consequences of broadcast technology, multiplied by cable and satellite transmission, can no longer be ignored. These consequences increasingly answer to McLuhan's description of them. A new world of violent and unreflective tribalism, whether represented by Los Angeles street gangs or armies in Bosnia, has been traced directly to the decline of literacy and the ascendancy of television by such scholars as Barry Sanders, the American author of the 1994 book A Is for Ox: Violence, Electronic Media, and the Silencing of the Written Word. *Sanders's book comes in the wake of other works by such noted scholars and critics as Neil Postman of New York University and Walter Ong of St. Louis University, substantiating the McLuhan thesis about the effects of broadcast media. These scholars underline McLuhan's notion, for example, that literacy—especially when amplified by print—is not simply a different way of absorbing information but a different way of relating to the world, to others, and to oneself. If electronic technology is indeed effacing centuries-old habits of literacy, then there is no better source for understanding the meaning of this effacement than the work of McLuhan.* ⊙

Today's environment is fertile ground for discovering McLuhan. He loved the maelstrom, the whirling vortex. He used Edgar Allen Poe's *Maelstrom* as a metaphor to describe the kind of media surround that constantly keeps us activated and mesmerized by change, and so I think he would be in love with this decade in terms of it giving him a constant repertoire of topics to discuss and to analyze. But whether from the standpoint of his deepest values he would love this time—probably not, because he would feel that certain traditional values are eroding. The use of TV commercials in the classroom, and the increasing commercialization of the academy and of parts of traditional learning, and the erasure of open-minded independence—*that* he would have detested. He loved the individual, iconoclastic maverick's mask that he wore. And so, yes, it would have been the best of times and, yes, it would have been the worst of times for McLuhan. And were he alive—although no one can put words in his mouth—he would be feasting on all the ground to critique but fasting from the stimulus of sensory overload, and especially from the artificial and increasingly synthetic world in which we live. **Tom Cooper**

He's not to everybody's taste and he never will be. He did not make things easy for the reader. If the medium is the message, he said, the user is the content, and sometimes the user doesn't work very hard. Now that's a harsh thing to say, especially in our day and age when everything is supposed to be so reader-friendly. You're not supposed to have to think or move a brain cell. This wasn't McLuhan's approach. His approach was, I'm going to give you these juxtapositions, I'm going to give you these erudite references. You've got to do some of the work to put it together, to test it out. He wasn't giving you gospel; he was giving you some tools for thinking about what's going on. It was up to you to apply them, as it's up to us now that he's gone to apply and keep testing some of what he was talking about. **Liss Jeffrey**

At what point is man going to recognize that this power of innovation may have to be restrained and that just as economically it may not be desirable to grow indefinitely, so that technologically it may not be necessary or desirable to innovate indefinitely? We're the first culture in the history of the world that ever regarded innovation as a friendly act.

Marshall McLuhan, *Marshall McLuhan with A. F. Knowles,* York University Instructional Services Video, 1971

Sensorium

Today, in America, there is a revolutionary attitude expressed as much in our attire as in our patios and small cars. For a decade and more, women's dress and hairstyles have abandoned visual for iconic—or sculptural and tactual—stress. Like toreador pants and gaiter stockings, the beehive hairdo is also iconic and sensuously inclusive, rather than abstractly visual. In a word, the American woman for the first time presents herself as a person to be touched and handled, not just to be looked at. While the Russians are groping vaguely towards visual consumer values, North Americans are frolicking amidst newly discovered tactile, sculptural spaces in cars, clothes, and housing. For this reason, it is relatively easy for us now to recognize clothing as an extension of the skin. In the age of the bikini and of skin diving, we begin to understand the castle of our skin as a space and world of its own. Gone are the thrills of striptease. Nudity could be naughty excitement only for a visual culture that had divorced itself from the audile-tactile values of less-abstract societies. As late as 1930, four-letter words made visual on the printed page seemed portentous. Words that most people used every hour of the day became as frantic as nudity when printed. Most four-letter words are heavy with tactile-involving stress. For this reason, they seem earthy and vigorous to visual man. So it is with nudity. To backward cultures still embedded in the full gamut of sense-life, not yet abstracted by literacy and industrial visual order, nudity is merely pathetic. The Kinsey Report on the sex life of the male expressed bafflement that peasants and backward peoples did not relish marital or boudoir nudity. Khrushchev did not enjoy the cancan dance provided for his entertainment in Hollywood. Naturally not. That sort of mime of sense involvement is meaningful only to long-literate societies. Backward peoples approach nudity, if at all, with the attitude we have come to expect from our painters and sculptors—the attitude made up of all the senses at once. To a person using the whole sensorium, nudity is the richest possible expression of structural form. But to the highly visual and lopsided sensibility of industrial societies, the sudden confrontation with tactile flesh is heady music, indeed. Marshall McLuhan, *Understanding Media*, 1964

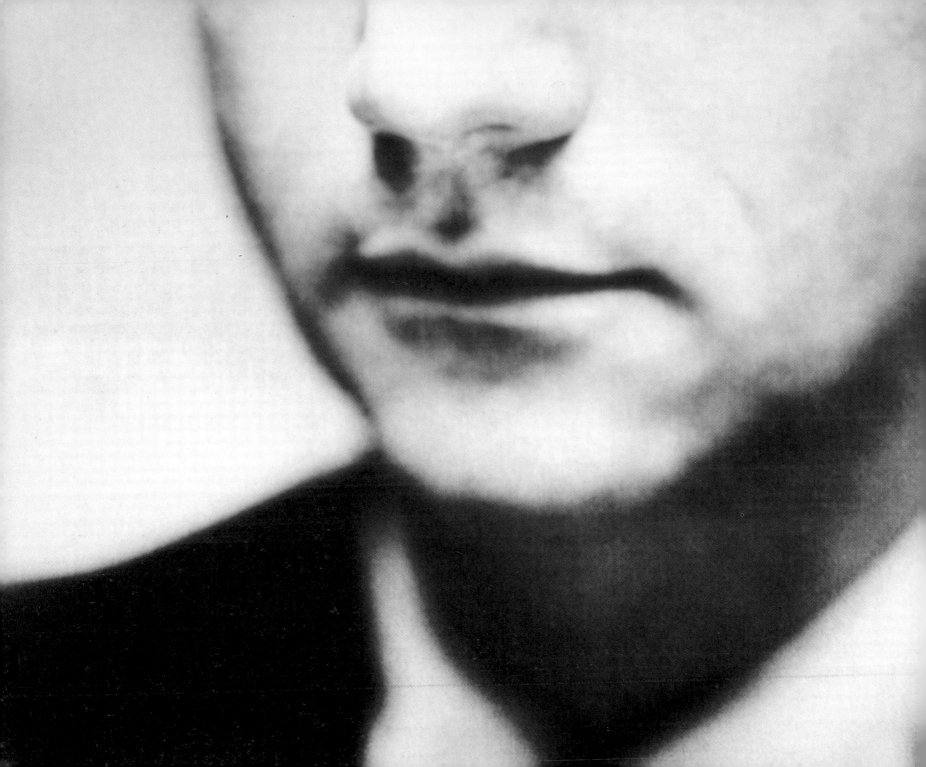

Pyromaniac
Of The Imagination

Around '68 or so when he was beginning to get shat on a lot and he was also going a little crazy himself, he was playing around with a 16mm or 8mm camera, down on the floor shooting pictures of his cats and then investing those pictures with a lot of significance that a whole lot of people couldn't quite perceive, which is what poets do. But I think this is an oversimplification of this particular poet. His poetry impacted on us, we loved it, but we said it was socio-economic cultural analysis. We tried to analyze it and it didn't stand up. Then we got mad at him; we said he was full of baloney. We rejected him. Now we look back at him and say he just made us think of stuff we would never have thought of before. And I think the more that that thinking is invested in poetic appetite, the more people are going to be able to say he left us with a great legacy. In my eulogy at his funeral I said he was a pyromaniac of the imagination starting prairie fires over our intellectual landscapes. **Patrick Watson**

Heaven

If I could speak to McLuhan in some heavenly situation, and I only had a minute to see him again, after I asked him how things are going, of course, I think I would tell him that what he did when he was here was extremely significant, that it opened up new pathways to thinking about media, and that there are thousands of young people now, in both the academic world, and in the communications industry, who think differently about what they're doing because he lived. So I'd say, "Thanks Marshall, go back to heaven." **Neil Postman**

Today

in the electronic age of instantaneous communication, I believe that our survival, and at the very least our comfort and happiness, is predicated on understanding the nature of our new environment, because unlike previous environmental changes, the electric media constitute a total and near instantaneous transformation of culture, values and attitudes. This upheaval generates great pain and identity loss, which can be ameliorated only through a consciousness of its dynamics. If we understand the revolutionary transformations caused by new media, we can anticipate and control them; but if we continue in our self-induced subliminal trance, we will be their slaves.

Marshall McLuhan, "Making Contact with Marshall McLuhan," interview by Louis Forsdale, 1974

Tom Cooper worked as an assistant to Marshall McLuhan at the Centre for Culture and Technology at the University of Toronto from 1974 to 1979. Today, Cooper is a professor of mass communications at Emerson College in Boston. He is a playwright, filmmaker, and the author of numerous books, including several about McLuhan.

Contributors

John Fraser is one of Canada's most influential men of letters. He is a former editor of *Saturday Night* magazine and was a critic, columnist, and foreign correspondent for the Toronto *Globe and Mail*. He is the author of several books, including *The Chinese: Portrait of a People, Telling Tales, Private View*, and *Stolen China*.

Robert Fulford is one of Canada's best-known journalists. Currently a columnist for the Toronto *Globe and Mail*, he was editor of *Saturday Night* magazine for nineteen years. Fulford hosted many CBC Television shows and is the author of *Accidental City: The Transformation of Toronto*.

Liss Jeffrey is a senior research associate at the McLuhan Program in Culture and Technology at the University of Toronto. A former journalist, Jeffrey is acting director of the MZTV Museum of Television in Toronto.

Derrick de Kerckhove is director of the McLuhan Program in Culture and Technology at the University of Toronto. De Kerckhove was an associate of the Centre for Culture and Technology from 1972 to 1980, and worked with McLuhan for more than ten years. He is the author of several books, including *Skin of Culture: Investigating the New Electronic Reality*.

Lewis Lapham is the editor of *Harper's* magazine, a position he has held since 1975. Lapham has written several books, including *Money and Class in America* and *Imperial Masquerade*. He wrote the introduction for The MIT Press's 1994 reissue of McLuhan's *Understanding Media: The Extensions of Man*.

Robert Logan is a University of Toronto physics professor and communications theorist. A student, friend, and colleague of Marshall McLuhan, Logan coauthored several papers and books with him in the late 1970s. Logan is the author of *The Alphabet Fffect* and *The Fifth Language*.

Philip Marchand was a student of McLuhan's at the University of Toronto. He is an award-winning magazine writer and the author of several books, including *Marshall McLuhan: The Medium and the Messenger*, the first full-length biography of McLuhan. He is currently a book columnist for *The Toronto Star*.

Eric McLuhan, the eldest son of Marshall McLuhan, collaborated with his father on *City as Classroom: Understanding Language and Media* and *Laws of Media: The New Science*. McLuhan holds a PhD in literature from the University of Dallas and has taught at universities in Canada and the U.S. He is a frequent lecturer and a partner in McLuhan & Davis Communications in Toronto.

Camille Paglia is the controversial author of *Sexual Personae: Art and Decadence from Nefertiti to Emily Dickinson* and *Sex, Art and American Culture: Essays*. Paglia graduated with a PhD from Yale University and is now a professor of humanities at the College of Performing Arts in Philadelphia.

Neil Postman is a communications professor at New York University. Hailed as "the new Marshall McLuhan," Postman has written extensively about the effects of television and other electronic media on culture. He is the author of many books, including *Amusing Ourselves to Death* and *Technopoly*.

Louis Rossetto is the cofounder and editor/publisher of *Wired* magazine, a San Francisco-based monthly on the digital revolution, which he launched in January 1993. Marshall McLuhan is the magazine's patron saint.

Frank Zingrone is a professor of communications and a senior scholar at York University in Toronto. Zingrone was a student, colleague, and friend of McLuhan, and he continues to research the theories of McLuhan and Harold Innis. Zingrone is the coeditor of the books *Who Was Marshall McLuhan?* and *Essential McLuhan*.

Patrick Watson, former chairman of the Canadian Broadcasting Corporation, is one of Canada's most distinguished writers and broadcasters. Born and educated in Toronto, Watson is an actor, writer, and producer for television and radio. He produced and hosted *This Hour Has Seven Days*, *Witness to Yesterday*, and *Heritage Minutes*.

Acknowledgements

In large part, this book grew out of the CD-ROM, *Understanding McLuhan*, which was produced at Southam Interactive. We owe much gratitute to those who agreed to be interviewed about Marshall McLuhan for the project: thanks to Tom Cooper, John Fraser, Robert Fulford, Liss Jeffrey, Derrick de Kerckhove, Lewis Lapham, Robert Logan, Philip Marchand, Eric McLuhan, Camille Paglia, Neil Postman, Louis Rossetto, Patrick Watson, and Frank Zingrone for sharing their memories of him. We would like to extend our thanks to all those who assisted in collecting and creating material for the CD-ROM, in particular Wayne McPhail, former director of Southam InfoLab, and Wilson Southam, former chairman of the Research and Development Committee, Southam Inc., who provided invaluable leadership and guidance. Thanks also to the members of the CD-ROM production team Dan Beer, Dan Clark, Maxine Wright, Bruno Leps, Russ Montgomery, and Dale Port; and to Sheila Turcon, Barbara Ledger, and Judy Donnelly for their research assistance. All of your efforts in creating *Understanding McLuhan* helped lay the foundation for this book.

Special thanks go to Prentice Hall Canada and acquisitions editor Sara Borins, who approached us with the idea for this book. Her contribution and the editorial and research assistance of Paula Thiessen, Anne-Marie Sorrenti, and Marijke Leupen are much appreciated. This book would also not exist without the collaboration of Alison Hahn and Nigel Smith of Hahn Smith Design, and the assistance of Dieter Janssen; we thank them for their unrelenting efforts in creating an exceptional design for this book. Thanks also to Laas Turnbull for copyediting this work and to Richard Hunt of Archetype for his typesetting expertise.

We also have tremendous appreciation for all those who offered their images for use in this book; they include photographers Ed Chin, Steven Evans, Judy Geher, Gabor Jurina, Rose Kallal, Kevin McBride, Matthew McCarthy, Greg Pacek, Charles Pachter, Hill Peppard, Nicole Rivelli, and Matthew Scrivens; artists Brian Boigon, Jean-Claude & Christo, Barbara Kruger, and Danny Tisdale; architects Nicholas Grimshaw and Partners Limited, and Jean Nouvel; Avi Lewis; and Toronto-based Student On-Site Solutions Inc. for the use of its "Help" computer image.

We sincerely express our gratitude to Corinne and Eric McLuhan, and to Matie Molinaro, who generously permitted us to look for research on Marshall McLuhan in their homes, offices, and personal archives. We also recognize Professor George Sanderson and Frank Macdonald of the Herbert Marshall McLuhan Foundation in Antigonish, Nova Scotia, for their assistance in researching McLuhan's writings. Marshall McLuhan's long-standing colleague Louis Forsdale was most helpful in his contribution of photos and audiotapes. The Canadian Broadcasting Corporation provided extensive McLuhan radio and television archival material; Geoffrey Hopkinson (CBC Visual Resource) deserves particular recognition for his dedicated assistance. For their help in arranging and filming the On McLuhan interviews from which the book's reminiscences on Marshall McLuhan were drawn, we would like to thank Andrew Heintzman, Evan Solomon, Mark Hyland, Duncan Wilson, and Nick de Pencier of *Shift* magazine; Barton Weiss of the Video Association of Dallas kindly provided transcripts of interviews with Tom Cooper and Camille Paglia. We are also grateful to Philip Marchand for his essay on McLuhan. Finally, a special thanks to Marni Flaherty for her support throughout this project.

Paul Benedetti and Nancy DeHart
August 1996

Sources

On McLuhan

Interviews with John Fraser, Robert Fulford, Liss Jeffrey, Derrick de Kerckhove, Lewis Lapham, Robert Logan, Philip Marchand, Eric McLuhan, Neil Postman, Louis Rossetto, Patrick Watson, and Frank Zingrone were all conducted between September 1994 and May 1995 by Andrew Heintzman, Mark Hyland, Nick de Pencier, Evan Solomon, and Duncan Wilson of *Shift* magazine in conjunction with Southam New Media, Toronto. Interviews with Tom Cooper and Camille Paglia were excerpted from transcripts of the film *Rewinding Into the Future: Massaging Marshall McLuhan*, directed by Barton Weiss. Video Association of Dallas, 1993.

By McLuhan

Books

The Mechanical Bride: Folklore of Industrial Man. New York: Vanguard Press, 1951.
The Gutenberg Galaxy: The Making of Typographic Man. New York: McGraw-Hill, 1962.
Understanding Media: The Extensions of Man. New York: McGraw-Hill, 1964.
The Medium is the Massage: An Inventory of Effects. With Quentin Fiore and Jerome Agel. New York: Bantam, 1907.
Take Today: The Executive as Dropout. With Barrington Nevitt. New York: Harcourt Brace Jovanovich, 1972.
Laws of Media: The New Science. With Eric McLuhan. Toronto: University of Toronto Press, 1988.

Articles

"At the moment of Sputnik the planet becomes a global theatre in which there are no spectators but only actors." *Journal of Communications*, Winter 1974, 45-58.
"Violence of the Media." *Canadian Forum.* September 1976, 9-12.
"A Last Look at the Tube." *New York*, 3 April 1978, 45.
"Living at the Speed of Light." *Maclean's*, 7 January 1980, 32-3.

Conference Speeches

"What fundamental changes are foreshadowed in the prevailing patterns of educational organization and methods of instruction by the revolution in electronics?" Speech at the fourteenth National Conference on Higher Education, Chicago, 3 March 1959.

Speech at the Conference on Management Information Systems, San Francisco, 1971.

Print Interviews

"Marshall McLuhan: The Man Who Infuriates the Critics," interview by Thomas P. McDonnel. *U.S. Catholic*, March 1966, 27-32.
"Conversations with Marshall McLuhan," interview by Gerald Emanuel Stearn. *Encounter*, June 1967, 50-58.
"*Playboy* Interview: Marshall McLuhan," interview by Eric Norden. *Playboy*, March 1969, 53-74 and 158.
"Electric Consciousness and the Church" interview by Herbert Hoskins. *The Listener*, 26 March 1970, 383-396.
"Making Contact with Marshall McLuhan," 1974 interview by Professor Louis Forsdale. In *Electric Media*, 148-158. New York: Harcourt, Brace, Jovanovich, 1974.
"Marshall McLuhan," 1972 interview by Willem L. Oltmans. In *On Growth: The Crisis of Exploding Population and Resource Depletion*, edited by Willem L. Oltmans, 71-77. New York: Capricorn Books, 1974.

Media Interviews

Take Thirty, CBC Television, 1 April 1965.
This Hour Has Seven Days, CBC Television, 8 May 1966.
"McLuhan on McLuhanism" Channel 13 WNDT Educational Broadcasting Corporation, 15 May 1966. Also published in "A McLuhan Montage." *School Library Journal*, April 1967, 39-41.
Telescope Revisited, "McLuhan is the Message." CBC Television, 20 July 1967.
The Best of Ideas, "The Marfleet Lectures." CBC Radio, 29 May and 12 June 1967.
The Seven O'Clock Show, CBC Television, 16 October 1967.
W5, CTV Television, 26 January and 18 May 1969.
Ideas, "Marshall McLuhan Gets Processed." CBC Radio, 2 December 1969.
The New Majority with Ed Fitzgerald, "A Conversation with Marshall McLuhan." CBC Television, 25 August 1970.
Marshall McLuhan with A.F. Knowles, York University Instructional Services Video, York University Technology Centre, 1971.

Other Sources

"McLuhan Probes," reprinted from *The Antigonish Review*, edited by George Sanderson. 74-75: summer-autumn 1988.

Matie Molinaro, Corinne McLuhan, and William Toye, editors. *Letters of Marshall McLuhan*. Toronto: Oxford University Press, 1987.

Unpublished articles from the archives of the Herbert Marshall McLuhan Foundation.

Image Credits

The publisher has made every effort to obtain proper credit information for all images used in this work. Any omission or error in image accreditation is inadvertent and will be corrected in subsequent editions of the work.

Opening Photographs

Global Village

Violence and Identity

Aquisitions editor and editorial director: Sara Borins
Creative services manager: Jan Coughtrey
Assistant editor: Paula Thiessen
Editorial assistance: Anne-Marie Sorrenti
Copy editor: Laas Turnbull
Production editor: Julie Preston

Designed by Hahn Smith Design with Dieter Janssen
Typeset by Richard Hunt at Archetype, Toronto
Set in Folio, Beton and Rockwell
Folio was designed by Konrad Bauer and
Walter Baum in 1962
Beton was designed by Heinrich Jost in 1930
Rockwell was designed by F. H. Pierpoint in 1934